CUBA

in Pictures

VGS

Kumari Campbell

Lerner Publications Company

Contents

INTRODUCTION 4

THE LAND 8

► Major Landforms. Rivers and Lakes. Climate. Flora and Fauna. Natural Resources. The Environment. Havana. Other Cities.

HISTORY AND GOVERNMENT 18

► The Conquistadores. Gatekeeper of the New World. Trade and Prosperity. Slavery and Revolt. The Second War of Independence. Independence at Last. The Batista Regime. The People's Revolution. Tensions with the United States. Postrevolutionary Cuba. Government.

THE PEOPLE 36

► Ethnic Groups. Standard of Living. Health and Social Services. Education.

Website address: www.lernerbooks.

Lerner Publications Company
A division of Lerner Publishing Group
241 First Avenue North
Minneapolis, MN 55401 U.S.A.

web enhanced @ www.vgsbooks.com

CULTURAL LIFE   44

▶ Religion. Holidays and Festivals. Literature.
Music and Dance. Visual Arts. Architecture.
Sports. Food.

THE ECONOMY   56

▶ Tourism. Sugar. Mining. Agriculture.
Manufacturing. Foreign Trade. Transportation.
The Future.

FOR MORE INFORMATION

▶ Timeline   66
▶ Fast Facts   68
▶ Currency   68
▶ Flag   69
▶ National Anthem   69
▶ Famous People   70
▶ Sights to See   72
▶ Glossary   73
▶ Selected Bibliography   74
▶ Further Reading and Websites   76
▶ Index   78

Library of Congress Cataloging-in-Publication Data

Campbell, Kumari.
        Cuba in pictures / by Kumari Campbell.
           p.   cm. — (Visual geography series)
        Includes bibliographical references and index.
        Contents: The land—History and government—The people—Cultural life—The economy.
        ISBN: 0-8225-1167-3 (lib. bdg. : alk. paper)
        1. Cuba—Juvenile literature. [1. Cuba.] I. Title. II. Series: Visual geography series (Minneapolis, Minn.)
        F1758.5.C36 2005
        972.9106'4'0222—dc22   2003026936

Manufactured in the United States of America
1 2 3 4 5 6 - JR - 10 09 08 07 06 05

INTRODUCTION

Cuba's strategic location as a gateway to the Americas has played an important role in the nation's development since its early days. Cuba is an island nation that lies in the Caribbean Sea, between the Atlantic Ocean and the Gulf of Mexico, south of the U.S. Florida Keys and east of Mexico's Yucatán Peninsula. The country's name comes from the word Cubanacán, meaning "central place" in Arawakan, the language used by the Taino, the last native people to inhabit Cuba. By the time the Spanish arrived in 1492, various groups of Arawak Indians had already lived on the island for several thousand years.

Much of Cuba's recent history was shaped by four centuries of Spanish colonization beginning in the early 1500s. Since the late 1950s, the nation has been dominated by the long-standing dictatorship of Fidel Castro, who came to power as a result of the Cuban revolution. Under his leadership, Cuba is the only Communist state in the Western world. A Communist system of government seeks to

share the resources and wealth of a country equally among all its citizens, through government ownership and distribution. Other Communist governments have fallen, but Castro remains firmly committed to this system.

Castro's embrace of Communist theories brought him into conflict with the anti-Communist United States early in his regime. The United States imposed a trade embargo on Cuba in 1961, forbidding trading partners of the United States to trade with Cuba. The embargo has remained in place ever since, and U.S. ports will not permit entry to ships that have visited Cuban ports. Unable to do business with its former trading partners of the democratic world, Cuba formed an alliance with the former Soviet Union and other Communist countries. Over the years, this alliance grew, providing a much-needed boost to the Cuban economy. The Soviet Union not only became Cuba's most important trading partner but also influenced social and cultural aspects of Cuban society.

As the economy improved, the Cuban government was able to spend more money on services such as housing, transportation and highway construction, community services, and food and household products for its citizens. But the collapse of the Soviet Union in 1991 led to a severe slump in the Cuban economy. In the period that followed, the government imposed drastic economic restraints on all Cubans, reduced spending on social services, and rationed food and other products, limiting the amount of these items that people could purchase.

Despite adversities, this island nation of more than eleven million people has a vibrant and harmonious culture. Cuba is a racially diverse country, with people of Spanish, African, and Chinese ancestry. Together they have survived past difficulties and continue to face economic and political struggles.

At the beginning of the revolution, the majority of Cubans supported Castro's ideas and plans for the future. But social, economic, and political hardships have left many Cubans disillusioned and frustrated. They wonder how much longer they will have to wait before they can enjoy the freedoms and lifestyles of other developed nations.

Meanwhile, the standoff between Cuba and the United States continues. Castro refuses to turn away from his strict Communist ideology, and in 2004 U.S. president George W. Bush tightened the trade embargo even further. The new restrictions angered many Cubans and Cuban Americans, especially the younger generation of Cuban Americans, who have a less rigid stance against the Castro regime. The goal of the embargo—to bring about Castro's downfall by depriving his government of dollars from U.S. tourists and goods—hasn't been achieved. Many observers expect the United States to loosen trade restrictions in the coming years.

If the embargo is eased, what will that mean for Cuba's future? Will increased trade with the United States and its allies bring positive or negative changes, or both? As Cuba moves into the twenty-first century, will the ideals of Castro's revolution survive? These are key questions confronting this small but prominent nation.

THE LAND

The crocodile-shaped island of Cuba is situated at the gateway to the Gulf of Mexico. Cuba, along with Jamaica, Hispaniola (an island made up of the nations of Haiti and the Dominican Republic), and Puerto Rico, form a chain of islands called the Greater Antilles. The islands stretch from east to west, separating the Caribbean Sea from the Atlantic Ocean. Dubbed the Pearl of the Antilles for its beauty, Cuba is 750 miles (1,200 kilometers) long, and on average 60 miles (100 km) wide. Cuba lies 90 miles (145 km) south of the Florida Keys and 130 miles (200 km) east of Mexico's Yucatán Peninsula. With an area of 44,218 square miles (114,524 sq. km), Cuba is approximately the size of the state of Pennsylvania.

◉ Major Landforms

Most of the central expanse of Cuba consists of flat or gently rolling land. With a base of limestone, the northern coastline tends to be steep and rocky, with coral reefs jutting out over the ocean. The most mountainous areas are in the extreme south and east and the south-central

region of the island. Together these areas account for approximately 25 percent of Cuba's landmass. The highest point on the island, Pico Turquino (6,540 feet; 1,993 meters), is in the rugged and wild Sierra Maestra range in southern Cuba. The Sierra del Escambray range in central Cuba is no higher than 3,740 feet (1,140 m).

The mountainous region in western Cuba, known as the Cordillera de Guaniguanico, includes the Sierra de los Órganos and Sierra del Rosario ranges, both about 2,300 feet (700 m) in height. These ranges consist mostly of low hills interspersed with individual mountains called *mogotes*, which look completely different from the surrounding hills. The limestone outcroppings rise abruptly from the ground, with sheer, vertical sides. The exteriors are sparsely covered with vegetation, while the interiors contain numerous caves and underground streams.

Also included in Cuban territory are about 1,600 offshore islands. Except for the 900-square-mile (2,330-sq.-km) Isla de la Juventud (Isle of Youth), they are tiny, uninhabited islets that ring the main island of

As an island nation, Cuba has miles of **beautiful beaches.** Cuba's tropical climate means beachgoers can enjoy sun and sand year-round. Visit www.vgsbooks.com for links to detailed information on Cuba's weather.

Cuba. The country's 3,570-mile (5,750-km) coastline offers 289 beaches, many of them considered among the world's most spectacular. Cuba has more than two hundred bays, many of which have provided superior natural harbors since the nation's early years.

Rivers and Lakes

Cuba lacks large rivers and lakes. Its longest river, the Cauto, flows 213 miles (343 km) through Granma province in the south. The river is not deep or wide enough to be navigated by vessels other than small boats. Other major rivers are the Zaza and the Sagua la Grande, both in central Cuba.

Although Cuba has no large lakes, the island's limestone bedrock contains a limitless supply of groundwater, with many underground rivers that empty into the ocean. Cubans have built hundreds of reservoirs to provide irrigation and drinking water.

Climate

Cuba has a pleasant subtropical climate, which is influenced year-round by the Northeast Trade Winds—winds that blow from the tropic of Cancer south toward the equator. Instead of hot and cold seasons, Cuba has dry and rainy seasons. The rainy season runs from May to October, while November through April are the dry months. Temperatures generally stay mild, varying from 72°F (22°C) during February, the coolest month, to 81°F (27°C) during the warmest months of July and August. The eastern part of the island tends to be slightly warmer than the western part, except in the mountain ranges.

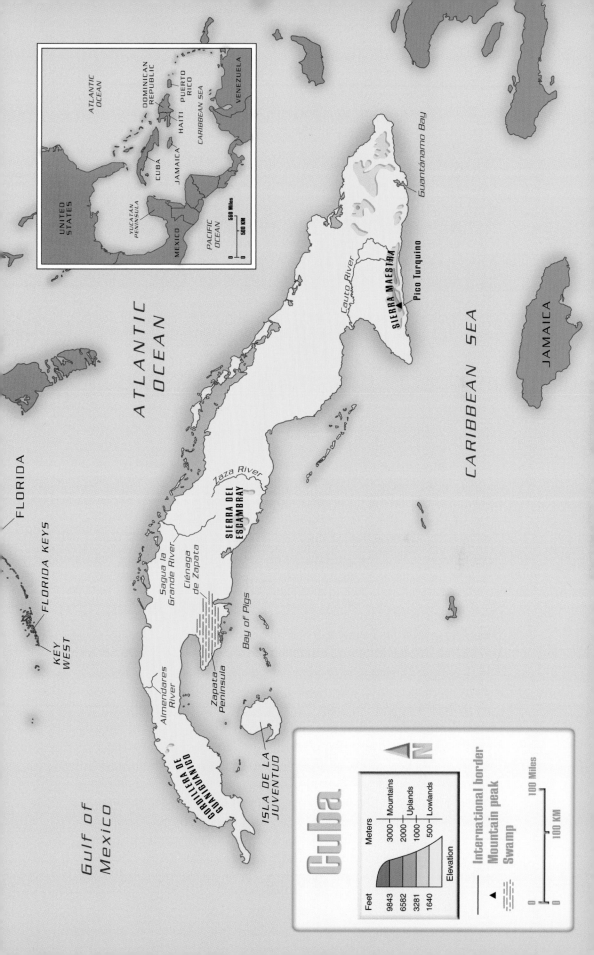

ATLANTIC
OCEAN

ATLANTIC OCEAN

DOMINICAN REPUBLIC
HAITI
PUERTO RICO
CARIBBEAN SEA
VENEZUELA

CUBA

JAMAICA

UNITED STATES

YUCATAN PENINSULA

MEXICO

PACIFIC OCEAN

500 Miles
500 KM

Guantánamo Bay

Cauto River

SIERRA MAESTRA

Pico Turquino

CARIBBEAN SEA

JAMAICA

FLORIDA

FLORIDA KEYS

KEY WEST

Gulf of Mexico

Zaza River

SIERRA DEL ESCAMBRAY

Sagua la Grande River

Ciénaga de Zapata

Bay of Pigs

Almendares River

Zapata Peninsula

ISLA DE LA JUVENTUD

CORDILLERA DE GUANIGUANICO

Cuba

N

Meters

3000 — Mountains
2000 — Uplands
1000 — Lowlands
500

Elevation

Feet
9843
6582
3281
1640

International border
Mountain peak
Swamp

100 Miles
100 KM

Average summer rainfall amounts to 42 inches (106 centimeters), with 12 inches (32 cm) in the winter. The eastern mountains receive more rainfall than the rest of the island. During the hurricane season (June to November), western Cuba is prone to damage from these fierce tropical storms, which produce heavy rains accompanied by winds of up to 155 miles per hour (250 km/hr). Hurricanes form in the Atlantic Ocean east of the Lesser Antilles (a chain of small islands that form a north-south line between Puerto Rico and the north coast of Venezuela), and then intensify as they move in a northwesterly direction over Cuba.

Flora and Fauna

Cuba's climate supports a range of vegetation types across the island. More than eight hundred species of plants flourish in Cuba, and many of them are native to the island. Tropical rain forests in the lower altitudes of the Sierra Maestra form the most densely forested areas on the island. The low plains that make up the central part of Cuba have mostly been cleared for crop and livestock farming. Low-lying swampy areas, particularly on the southern coast, are forested with mangroves. These unique coastal trees thrive in salt water and help stabilize the shoreline against erosion, the wearing away of the land by the ocean's constant wave action. The Ciénaga de Zapata, a swamp that covers the entire Zapata Peninsula on the southern coast, is the largest mangrove growth on the island.

Pines grow plentifully in the westernmost Pinar del Río province. Ebony and mahogany are rain forest trees that are much prized for their beautiful wood. Of the ninety-seven varieties of palms native to Cuba, the most common is the royal palm, which is the national tree. Every part of the stately tree is used: the leaves, bark, and termite-resistant wood for building materials; the tender center, or heart, as food; and the fruit for its oil, which is extracted to make soap and pig feed. Other common palms include coconut and betel. The belly palm, named for its round middle, grows only in Cuba. The cork palm, found only in western Cuba, is an extremely rare species that dates back to the Cretaceous period 65 to 135 million years ago.

The flame tree, common throughout Cuba, is a picturesque sight with its bright red and orange blooms among spreading branches. Other flowering trees and plants, including jacaranda, frangipani, magnolia, jasmine, gardenia, oleander, bougainvillea, and hundreds of orchid species, paint the island with bursts of color year-round.

Due to extensive use of land for agriculture, once-plentiful mammals such as deer, rabbits, and squirrels have all but disappeared, leaving the jutía (tree rat) and the bat as the most common indigenous

The stunning red flowers of the **flame tree** are set off against the lush green of Cuba's forests.

(native) land mammals in Cuba. Reptiles abound on the island, however, and include snakes, crocodiles, iguanas, lizards, and salamanders. Cuba's largest snake is the maja, a species of boa that can grow up to 13 feet (4 m) long. The Cuban crocodile has been saved from extinction by a breeding program in the Zapata Peninsula. Cuba is home to the alligator gar, an enormous fish that can grow up to 10 feet (3 m) long, may weigh 300 pounds (135 kilograms), and has two rows of large teeth. Manatees (seal-like marine mammals) and sea turtles live in Cuba's seas.

Cuban crocodile

Birds are the most plentiful wild creatures in Cuba. Among the more than 350 species that nest on the island are parrots, pelicans, cranes, egrets, flamingos, ibis, mockingbirds, nightingales, warblers, woodpeckers, and hummingbirds. Cuba's winter bird population includes migratory species that spend the summer months in North America. The most common bird habitats in Cuba are the Sierra Maestra, the Ciénaga de Zapata, and the western tip of Pinar del Río province.

Like the flowering plants, most birds in Cuba are extremely colorful, a trait that is common in tropical regions of the world. The striking tocororo, or Cuban trogon, is the national bird, chosen for its prominent red, blue, and white plumage, which mirrors the colors of the Cuban flag. Cuba is also home to the world's tiniest bird, the zunzuncito, or bee hummingbird. The male weighs just .07 ounces (2 grams). The female, which is slightly larger, lays two eggs each spring that are the size of tiny jelly beans. These birds' wings beat so rapidly as they hover over flowers feeding on nectar that they are invisible to the human eye.

Natural Resources

Cuba's most important natural resource is the land that is used to grow sugarcane and tobacco. These valuable crops are used to make the country's most important exports, sugar and cigars. The land also supports food crops for the country's own use.

Cuba is also rich in mineral deposits, particularly nickel, which is used in stainless steel and to make coins, knives, and other items. About 35 percent of the world's nickel deposits are contained within a short section of coastal land in northeastern Holguín province. Other important minerals found in Cuba are cobalt, chromite, copper, tungsten, manganese, and iron. The small nation also has significant petroleum deposits, and it produces enough fuel to meet the country's power needs. Yet the petroleum is not of a suitable quality to use as gasoline for cars. Therefore, Cuba still must import petroleum.

Another important resource is fish and seafood from the waters surrounding Cuba. Several ports around the island are used for fishing plentiful stocks of red snapper, muttonfish, tarpon, swordfish, bonito, barracuda, mackerel, marlin, and shark. However, these stocks are shrinking fast because the growing number of visitors to the island love to feast on seafood. In even greater danger are shellfish species, including lobster, crawfish, shrimp, crab, and oyster, which are even more popular with tourists.

The Environment

Because the Cuban government faces continuing challenges in trying to finance necessities such as food, health care, and education for its citizens, environmental issues are not a high priority. Air pollution is a serious problem in Cuba. Most of the island's motor vehicles are several decades old, and no controls are set on their emissions (substances discharged into the air). In addition, numerous factories and mining operations across the island contribute to the pollution.

Cuba's sea and land resources are under pressure due to increased fishing to feed tourists, as well as increased use of land for growing sugarcane, tobacco, and other crops. An even more danger-

Vintage cars such as this 1950s U.S. model are common in Cuba, but they contribute to air pollution.

Once beautiful old buildings in La Habana Vieja (Old Havana) suffer from disrepair.

ous assault on the land is the development of oceanfront tourist resorts, which damage the sensitive natural habitats of birds, marine life, and other wild animals. Other natural areas of the island are also in danger of being destroyed by the large numbers of tourists who flock there.

Havana

Havana, called La Habana in Spanish, is the national capital, the largest city in Cuba, and also the largest city in the Caribbean. Its population of 2.2 million people accounts for 19 percent of the nation's residents.

The town of San Cristóbal de la Habana (Havana's original name) was first established by the Spanish in 1514 on the southern coast, almost directly south of modern Havana. Shortly afterward, the city was moved to the banks of the Almendares River on the north coast, and in 1519 to its modern location to the east, at the mouth of the Havana harbor. Havana became the colony's capital in 1607. As the center of Spain's New World colonies, Havana shone with all the splendor of the empire. Walls enclosed the original city, and several forts protected it from invasion. No expense was spared as the Spanish built magnificent public buildings, churches, and private palaces.

In 1863 the city walls had to be demolished, as they could no longer contain the expanding urban center. In 1958 a 2,405-foot (733-m) tunnel was built under the harbor, letting the city spill over to the east

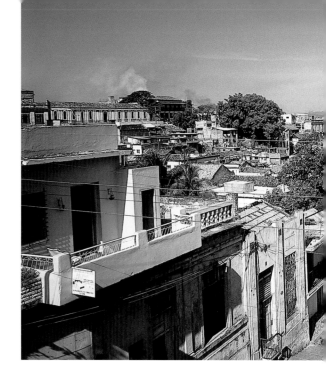

side of the harbor. Havana has since expanded to 278 square miles (720 sq. km) and is divided into 15 municipalities.

The old section of Havana, called La Habana Vieja, remains untouched. Since the revolution in 1959, the government has been unable to afford the upkeep and renovations needed to maintain the city's historic buildings. Approximately three hundred buildings collapse each year, and those still standing are badly deteriorated. In 1982 the United Nations Educational, Scientific, and Cultural Organization (UNESCO) declared La Habana Vieja a World Heritage Site. Since then, the Cuban government has embarked on a massive reconstruction program. Historic buildings are being carefully rebuilt according to their original design. The only change is the installation of modern electrical wiring, plumbing, and appliances.

Havana continues to be the center of government, commerce, education, research, culture, communications, and tourism in Cuba. It is also a major industrial center, producing electricity, metals, chemicals, ships, paper, textiles, cigars, and food. Havana has a petroleum refinery and is home to the largest fishing fleet in the nation. Despite difficult living conditions in the city, including a severe housing shortage, thousands of Cubans come to the capital each year in search of employment.

Other Cities

Santiago de Cuba, with a population of 440,000 people, is Cuba's second-largest city. As one of the original seats of colonial power, Santiago boasts a rich Spanish colonial architecture that, like Havana's, is in a state of decay. Santiago rivals Havana as a center of the arts. The city's cultural legacy dates from the arrival of a large

Santiago de Cuba is on the southeastern coast of Cuba. Terra-cotta rooftops are typical of the city's Spanish colonial architecture.

number of French refugees from Haiti following a slave uprising there in 1791. The French introduced opera and classical European music to Cuba. They also brought large numbers of African slaves to work on coffee, cotton, and sugarcane plantations, giving Santiago the largest Afro-Cuban population in Cuba. This, along with further Afro-Haitian immigration in the 1800s, led to development of a distinct African folk culture in the region, represented by Afro-Cuban music, drumming, and dance.

Santiago de Cuba has one of the three major harbors on Cuba's southern coast. The city's industries include the manufacturing of sugar, coffee, rum, textiles, furniture, and cement. Shipbuilding, electricity generation, and petroleum refining are other important local industries.

Cuba's third-largest city, Camagüey, with a population of 300,000 people, is one of the original seven settlements established by the Spanish between 1512 and 1514. As such, Camagüey has a similar colonial architecture and layout as Havana and Santiago. Camagüey is home to one of Cuba's largest universities. Other major cities in Cuba are the provincial capitals of Holguín, Santa Clara, and Cienfuegos.

Visit www.vgsbooks.com for links to websites with additional information about Cuba's cities and towns. You'll learn about the history, architecture, cultural events, population facts, and more.

HISTORY AND GOVERNMENT

The earliest-known inhabitants of the island of Cuba were believed to have arrived between 3500 and 2000 B.C. Experts disagree about the number and identity of these early peoples, but they generally agree that various nomadic groups moved to the Caribbean islands from South, Central, or North America, traveling in canoes from island to island. Two groups that are thought to have settled in Cuba were the Guanahatabey and the Ciboney, who were part of the larger Arawak group of people. The Arawaks were originally from South America and gradually moved north to the Antilles.

The Guanahatabey settled in western Cuba, while the Ciboney made their homes in the east. Both groups were peaceful fishers, hunters, and gatherers, and they lived undisturbed for hundreds of years. In about A.D. 1250, another group of Arawak Indians, called the Taino, fled to eastern Cuba from the islands of Puerto Rico and Hispaniola, where they were being terrorized by the fierce, warring Carib people. The Taino soon became the dominant group in Cuba.

The Taino people had a more advanced society than the other native groups in Cuba. The Taino lived in villages and grew yams, corn, pumpkins, peanuts, peppers, avocados, and tobacco. They created tools and religious statues of stone, wood, gourds, and bone; canoes from tree trunks; clay pottery; woven cotton fishnets and hammocks; and baskets and furniture from palm leaves and branches. The Taino lived in thatched huts called *bohíos* clustered around an open common area. They spoke Arawakan, the language that gave English such words as hammock, tobacco, and canoe.

The Conquistadores

On October 27, 1492, Italian explorer Christopher Columbus, known in Spain as Cristóbal Colón, landed on the largest island in the Caribbean Sea. Columbus claimed the island for King Ferdinand V and Queen Isabella I, the Spanish rulers who had financed his explorations. In his journals, Columbus described the island as "the most beautiful

The Arawaks were the most important Indian group in South America and the Caribbean during pre-Columbian times. The area was home to almost one hundred Arawakan tribes, including the Ciboney, and the Taino. Arawakan tribes still survive in Bolivia, Brazil, Colombia, Peru, and Venezuela.

land human eyes have ever seen." Upon his return two years later, the Taino greeted the Europeans with gifts.

The Taino soon learned that these visitors did not have friendly intentions. The Spanish captured and enslaved tribe members and transported some of them to other Spanish colonies, the territories that Spain was claiming for itself in North and South America and the Caribbean. In 1511 the Spanish began their conquest of Cuba, led by Diego Velázquez and his three hundred conquistadores, or conquerors. They landed near the southeastern tip of Cuba and established the settlement of Baracoa.

Within four years, Velázquez and his men, using Baracoa as a base, had established six other Cuban settlements: Bayamo, Trinidad, Sancti Spíritus, San Cristóbal de la Habana (Havana), Puerto Príncipe (later relocated to Camagüey), and Santiago de Cuba. The towns were laid out in the European style, on a rectangular grid with a central square dominated by a church. In 1515 Velázquez moved his headquarters to Santiago de Cuba, making it the colonial capital.

Spain's main interest in Cuba was gold. The conquistadores used the Taino as slaves in their gold mining and panning operations. But while Cuba was rich in mineral deposits, gold was not one of them. The Spanish shifted their attention to growing sugarcane and tobacco, products that were nearly as valuable as gold.

Spanish soldiers oversee **slaves mining for gold** in Cuba in the early 1500s.

Under the *encomienda* labor system, the Taino were forced to work on sugar and tobacco plantations for Spanish conquistadores in return for being fed and housed. They also were given religious instruction, even though they already had their own religion. The Spanish brought the Roman Catholic Christian faith to Cuba and to their other New World colonies. Beginning in the early 1500s, various groups of Spanish Catholic priests, such as Jesuits, Franciscans, and Dominicans, began converting the native peoples in the colonies to Catholicism.

Large numbers of Taino were slaughtered when they fought back. The harsh slave labor killed many others. Scores also died of diseases introduced to the island by Europeans. The Taino had no natural resistance (immunity) to illnesses such as smallpox, measles, and influenza. Within half a century, the Taino population had dwindled to fewer than 5,000 from the original 100,000 who inhabited the island. As the Taino population declined, the Spanish conquerors began to import African slaves to replace the Taino. The slaves belonged to several West African tribes, including the Bantu, the Congolese, the Dahoman, the Mandingo, and the Yoruba.

Gatekeeper of the New World

As Spain's colonies grew in number and importance, the Spanish rulers realized the strategic value of Cuba's location. Positioned at the crossroads of trade routes between Europe and the Americas, Cuba soon became an important center of transatlantic commerce. Spain allowed Cuba to trade only with a single port in Spain, however.

In 1526 Spain directed all its ships returning with treasures from the New World, as the Americas were known, to meet in the Havana harbor and sail together across the Atlantic Ocean to the Old World (Europe). As many as ninety ships laden with gold, silver, gems, and other valuable items would gather in Havana's harbor over the summer months. Then they would set off together across the Atlantic.

The primary reason for sailing in large groups was the considerable threat from pirates. Cuba's harbors, while useful for shipping, also offered hiding places for smugglers and pirates. The Isle of Youth, then known as the Isle of Pines, was a particularly popular hideout. In 1555 French pirate Jacques de Sores, using the Isle of Pines as a base, plundered several ships in the Havana harbor. To protect the city, the Spaniards built El Castillo de los Tres Reyes de Magos del Morro (El Morro) on the east side of the harbor and the Real Fuerza Castle on the west side.

Trade and Prosperity

While Spain's Caribbean colonies battled pirates, Spain faced other challenges in the Old World. When France went to war against Britain

During the 1700s, slaves and native peoples in Saint-Domingue protested the harsh treatment they endured from the European colonizers. A slave uprising *(above)* in the early 1800s forced French colonists to seek safety in Cuba.

and its allies in 1756, Spain sided with France. The conflict became known as the Seven Years' War.

In 1762 Havana was captured by the British, who occupied the city for eleven months. During the occupation, the British allowed Cuba to begin trading with all British North American colonies, including those that later became the United States of America. Trade in Cuba increased from fifteen Spanish ships visiting the island each year to seven hundred ships from many places.

Under the terms of the treaty that ended the Seven Years' War in 1763, Britain returned Cuba to Spain in exchange for Florida, which had been under French control. Spain let Cuba keep its new trading partners and also opened six more Spanish ports to Cuban trade in 1765, greatly boosting the island's trading power.

The late 1700s and early 1800s were prosperous years for Cuba. A slave uprising in the French section of Hispaniola, Saint-Domingue (which later became Haiti), sent about thirty thousand French colonists to Cuba in search of refuge. They brought with them steam-powered machinery that modernized the sugar industry. In 1795 the Spanish part of Hispaniola, Santo Domingo (later the Dominican Republic), came under French rule. Consequently, the Caribbean seat of Spanish government was moved to Cuba.

In 1801 the newly independent nation of Haiti invaded Santo Domingo, prompting thousands of Spanish people living there to move to Cuba. In 1803 even more Spanish and French colonists moved to Cuba from the United States after France sold the Louisiana Territory—

a huge portion of land west of the Mississippi River—to the United States. In 1818 Spain gave Cuba permission to trade freely with any world nation. These expanded trade opportunities, along with the influx of new colonists, provided a huge boost to Cuba's economy. As a result, many public and private buildings were built across the island.

Slavery and Revolt

By 1825 all of Spain's Central and South American colonies except Cuba and Puerto Rico had won their independence. Cuban slave owners feared that Cuba would be next to revolt and that independence would set off riots among the large numbers of African slaves in the colony.

In treaties signed between Britain and Spain in 1817 and 1835, Spain agreed to end slave trading (though not slave ownership) in its colonies. But the Spanish government didn't abide by the treaty. Spanish ships continued to carry slaves from Africa to meet the demand for laborers in Cuba's growing sugar industry. Finally, in 1865 and 1866, the Spanish government ended the slave trade. Unable to manage without their ready supply of new slave labor, landowners in Cuba brought in Chinese and Mexican laborers to work in the fields. But the new arrivals were not treated much better than the African slaves were.

Meanwhile, discontent was brewing among the criollos, Cuban-born citizens of Spanish descent. Cuba's economic prosperity had so far

Slaves move wagonloads of sugarcane through a **Cuban sugar plantation** in the 1860s.

largely benefited Spanish-born Cuban citizens, known as *peninsulares.* Many criollos resented the fact that their country was being governed by peninsulares acting on orders from Spain. Instead, they favored a system of local governance that would transfer more power into their hands. These resentments were widespread throughout rural Cuba, especially in the Oriente region, the easternmost part of the island.

In October 1868, Carlos Manuel de Céspedes, a criollo plantation owner from Oriente, led a rebel uprising in the eastern half of the colony. Having freed his own slaves, Céspedes demanded freedom for all of Cuba's slaves, as well as independence from Spain. The rebels, including Céspedes' freed slaves, fought bravely at first, capturing much of eastern Cuba. But as the conflict dragged on into a decade-long crusade, they lost their strength and will. Fearful of the powerful peninsulares in western Cuba, the rebels softened their initial demands for complete independence and removed Céspedes as commander.

The war, known as the Ten Years' War or the First War of Independence, ended in February 1878, when the Spanish authorities pardoned the rebels. More than 200,000 people lost their lives, and the Oriente region suffered tremendous destruction. Although Spain transferred a few more powers to Cuba, the penisulares still continued to rule the colony. Slavery remained legal in Cuba until 1886.

Ten years of war had weakened Cuba's economy. Investors from the United States seized the opportunity to purchase Cuban plantations and factories that had suffered bankruptcies. To support these powerful investors, the U.S. government removed almost all tariffs (taxes on imported goods) on Cuban products. The United States, already the largest importer of Cuban sugar, soon became its most important trading partner. With trade flourishing, Cuba prospered once more, but only the wealthy business owners benefited.

◉ The Second War of Independence

In the 1890s, a Cuban poet, essayist, and lawyer named José Martí began organizing another war for independence. Martí had been exiled to Spain for his anticolonial activities during the Ten Years' War and had then moved to New York City. He recruited two key veterans of the first war, Máximo Gómez and Antonio Maceo, to help him carry out the rebellion. Martí landed near Baracoa in Oriente province on April 11, 1895, beginning Cuba's Second War of Independence. But Martí's leadership was short lived. He died in battle on May 19, just five weeks after his arrival.

Martí's associates forged on ahead, this time heeding the mistakes of the First War of Independence. Rather than concentrating their efforts in eastern Cuba, they marched west, toward the power base of Havana, laying waste to everything in their path. The Spanish colonial government fought back just as ruthlessly. The result was the loss of thousands of lives and the devastation of Cuba's agriculture-based economy.

In early 1898, the United States sent the battleship USS *Maine* to Havana to protect U.S. citizens in Cuba. On February 15, the ship was blown up as it lay anchored west of the harbor. The Spanish government, the U.S. government, and the Cuban insurgents all accused each other of setting off the explosion, but the cause was never proven. Although Spain declared a cease-fire in the war with Cuba on April 9, the U.S. Congress, responding to strong public support for the Cuban rebels, called for Cuba's independence and demanded that Spain withdraw its armed forces from the island. On April 25, the United States declared war against Spain. The conflict became known as the Spanish-American War.

The war was quick and one-sided, as Spanish forces were ill prepared. Within a month, the United States had blockaded the Spanish fleet in Santiago de Cuba Bay. U.S. troops, including Theodore Roosevelt and his First Volunteer Cavalry, the Rough Riders, landed on the coast near Santiago de Cuba and advanced toward the city. The fighting lasted just a few weeks, and in July, Spanish forces surrendered to U.S. troops.

No Cubans were invited to witness the signing of the peace treaty between Spain and the United States in Paris, France, on December 10,

REMEMBER THE *MAINE!*

As Cuba struggled for independence from Spain during the 1890s, U.S. newspapers published sensationalized, wild stories of the horrors of Cuban life under Spanish rule. Led by newspaper owners Joseph Pulitzer and William Randolph Hearst, the journalism of the time helped propel the United States into a war with Spain.

After the sinking of the battleship *Maine* near Havana, Hearst ran a series of articles blaming the Spanish for the incident. He coined the phrase, "Remember the *Maine!* To hell with Spain," and helped whip up a frenzy of public support for the war.

According to a famous story, one of Hearst's illustrators, Frederic Remington, was sent to Havana to cover the Cuban rebellion. Finding nothing to report about, Remington requested permission to return. Hearst replied, "Please remain. You furnish the pictures and I'll furnish the war."

For links to more information on the destruction of the *Maine*, visit www.vgsbooks.com.

1898, which gave the United States control over Cuba. For the second time, Cubans had failed to win their independence.

Independence at Last

On January 1, 1899, Cuba's first U.S. governor assumed control. The rebels were disbanded. The peninsulares, however, were permitted to keep their government positions. In late 1900, the U.S. military government permitted certain Cubans—those who could read, those with property valued in excess of $250, and veterans of the rebel army—to elect delegates to draft a new constitution for Cuba.

Although the constitution gave Cuba partial independence, the United States added the Platt Amendment, which gave the United States some control over Cuba, including the right to intervene in Cuban affairs and to build a naval base on the island for U.S. defense purposes. At first, the delegates refused to accept these terms. But when it was made clear to them that Cuba's independence depended on the adoption of the Platt Amendment, they signed it.

The Platt Amendment to the Cuban Constitution gave the United States the right to build a naval base at Guantánamo Bay, in the southeastern corner of Cuba. In 1903 the base was built, and in 1934 the lease was extended for ninety-nine years (until 2033). Surrounded by barbed wire, the base has been used to hold people suspected of terrorism following the terrorist attacks of September 11, 2001, on the United States.

On May 20, 1902, Cuba made a fresh start as the Republic of Cuba. As the U.S. flag was lowered at the governor's palace, it was replaced by the single-starred, red, white, and blue flag of the new republic. But the new president, Tomás Estrada Palma, quickly ran into problems caused by the squabbling of Cuba's two main political parties, the Liberals and the Conservatives.

The two parties had been formed during the period between the two wars of independence. The Liberals called for immediate reform and complete independence, while the Conservatives were happy with the new republic and the Platt Amendment.

Eventually, Estrada Palma allied himself with the Conservatives, and the Liberals mounted an armed rebellion in response. The United States stepped in once more and occupied the island, this time from 1906 to 1909. This second U.S. occupation was followed by a series of short-lived, corrupt Cuban governments.

While Cuba struggled with political turmoil, it also careened through alternate bouts of prosperity and adversity triggered by the ups and downs of sugar prices. By 1933 worldwide depression, a severe business and economic downturn, had taken hold of Cuba. At the time, the regime of President Gerardo Machado, a Liberal who had been elected in 1925, was coming to an end after years of corruption and dictatorial rule. A U.S. mediator appointed a temporary president, but he was unable to control riots that broke out in Havana and other cities.

The Batista Regime

An army sergeant named Fulgencio Batista emerged from the chaos to lead a military revolt and form a new government. Commissioning himself as commander in chief of the armed forces with the rank of general, Batista installed a new president in 1934. Batista ruled the country from behind the scenes for six years. In 1940 he took over the presidency himself.

Corruption in the Cuban government reached unprecedented levels. Gambling and prostitution were allowed to flourish, and the money generated by these activities personally benefited Batista and his high-ranking government officials. All the while, Batista maintained good relations with the United States. He even convinced the U.S. government to cancel the Platt Amendment, an action that greatly endeared him to the people of Cuba. In 1944 Batista lost the presidency to Ramón Grau San Martín. Grau and his successor governed for two terms, but Batista returned in 1952 to overthrow the government, as he had done in 1934. This time he ruled as a dictator.

Fulgencio Batista (right, with dark hair at microphone) takes the oath of office to become president of Cuba in 1940.

During the 1940s and 1950s, tourism flourished in Cuba, which was a popular destination for U.S. visitors. But most Cubans remained poor, especially in the rural areas. Many people worked on sugarcane and tobacco farms and in sugar manufacturing factories. The work was hard, and the hours were long. Workers barely earned enough money to house and feed themselves and their families. They lived on rice and beans and wore tattered clothes. Often several families shared one small, cramped house. Most homes lacked running water and electricity, and access to health care was limited. Many people died from diseases that could have been cured with proper medication. Most children did not go to school.

With living conditions so dismal, the majority of Cubans resented the government. Widespread unrest set the stage for another revolution. An attempt came on July 26, 1953, when a young lawyer and former student revolutionary named Fidel Castro led an attack on the Moncada army barracks in Santiago. Although the uprising was a failure, it represented the first step toward revolution and propelled Castro to the forefront of the fight.

When his attack on Moncada failed, Castro was tried and imprisoned. During the trial, he delivered a famous five-hour speech in which he denounced the Batista dictatorship and appealed for reforms that would improve the lives of ordinary Cubans. Castro was sentenced to fifteen years in prison, but Batista bowed to public pressure and pardoned and released Castro and other political prisoners in 1955. Castro went to Mexico to plot his next action. There he met Ernesto "Che" Guevara, a revolutionary from Argentina who joined Castro and his fellow rebels as they planned their return to Cuba.

The People's Revolution

Within a year, Castro was ready to launch what he called the People's Revolution—a revolt by the common people against the small group who held power in Cuba. Castro and his supporters were angered that a minority of rich people governed the country. These few had access to money and power, while the majority of citizens remained poor and powerless. The revolutionaries were determined to change this system into one in which all Cubans, regardless of ethnic origin, religion, or occupation, would benefit from the country's resources. In such a classless society, all people would be equal, with the same rights, benefits, and responsibilities.

On December 2, 1956, Castro, Guevara, and eighty of their followers tried to land near Manzanillo in eastern Cuba. But they were met by Batista's forces. Many of the rebels were killed or captured, and others deserted the group. In the end, only twelve rebels remained. They fled to the Sierra Maestra.

Over the next two years, the rebels spread their cause from their mountain hideaway. The rebels' July 26th Movement, named for the date of Castro's first uprising, grew steadily. Castro's followers built a hospital and schools for the local residents. By early 1958, the rebels operated their own radio station, which Castro used to speak directly to the Cuban people, urging them to revolt.

In May 1958, Batista dispatched twelve thousand soldiers to eastern Cuba to capture the rebels. Following several months of fighting, the government forces were forced to withdraw. Soldiers who had been captured by the rebels were treated so well that many of them joined the rebellion. In August, Castro, his three main lieutenants—his brother Raúl, Che Guevara, and Camilo Cienfuegos—and many supporters fanned out across the island on a march toward Havana.

On January 1, 1959, Batista left Havana for the last time, choosing to flee to safety rather than be assassinated. He first went to the Dominican Republic and then to Portugal. A week later, Fidel Castro marched triumphantly into Havana, amidst the cheers and praise of a grateful nation.

Che Guevara (left) and Fidel Castro (right) led the People's Revolution against the Cuban ruling class in the 1950s. Visit www.vgsbooks.com for links to more information about Cuba's revolution.

CHE GUEVARA

Born in Argentina in 1928, Ernesto Guevara grew up in a middle-class family. After receiving a medical degree in 1953, he traveled extensively in Latin America. Appalled by the poverty and oppression he saw, he became determined to help fight for better conditions. He joined Fidel Castro and became a major figure in the People's Revolution. Guevara's Cuban friends nicknamed him Che, the Argentine expression for "hey," which he used frequently.

Guevara held many important positions in Castro's regime, including minister of industry. In 1966 he left Cuba to help liberate the people of Bolivia, but he was executed there the following year. His remains were returned to Cuba in 1997, where they were buried in Santa Clara.

A victorious Fidel Castro (center) took over the Cuban government in 1959. He has been in power ever since.

Tensions with the United States

On January 5, 1959, Manuel Urrutia, a judge sympathetic to the revolution, was appointed president of the Cuban republic's new government. This was primarily a ceremonial position, however. The real power lay with Fidel Castro, who assumed the position of prime minister.

As Castro took control, his main goal was to rescue Cuba's economy from dependence on a single commodity, sugar, which was traded to a single country, the United States. He believed that diversity in production and trade would serve Cuba better.

Castro was not overtly hostile toward his northern neighbor when he gained control of Cuba. This changed, however, as Castro began to put Communist ideas into practice in Cuba. Communism is a political and economic system based on the principle that all of a nation's resources should be held jointly by the people, or the government of the people. This ideology, or set of theories, conflicted with the United States' democratic principles and capitalist economic system, which emphasized private ownership of property.

In 1960 Castro nationalized (put under government ownership) nearly six thousand U.S. businesses. The United States in turn cut off diplomatic relations in early 1961 and banned its citizens from traveling to Cuba. The United States also imposed a trade embargo, cutting off all imports and exports between Cuba and the United States. As Cuba moved further from its American ties, it built closer relationships with other Communist countries, especially the Soviet Union (officially known as the Union of Soviet Socialist Republics, or USSR, of which Russia was the largest republic).

During this period, large numbers of Cubans—in particular, well-paid professionals and those who had held high-ranking government jobs during the Batista regime—left Cuba for the United States. They feared they would lose their freedom and possessions or that they would be jailed as political prisoners.

On April 17, 1961, a group of 1,400 Cuban exiles landed at the Bay of Pigs on the southwestern coast of Cuba. Supported by the United States, the exiles planned to invade the island. They expected other Cubans to join them and overthrow the Castro regime, but this didn't happen. The Cuban army was called out, and after about two hundred exiles had been killed, the rest surrendered. Later, about 1,200 prisoners were returned to the United States in exchange for $53 million in food and medicine.

The following year, Cuba asked the Soviet Union for military protection, fearing a possible U.S. invasion. The Soviets built secret missile bases in Cuba and began installing missiles carrying nuclear weapons aimed at the United States. In October 1962, after U.S. spy planes discovered the missile sites in Cuba, President John F. Kennedy ordered a blockade of Soviet ships carrying missiles to Cuba. He called on the Soviets to remove all missiles in Cuba and stop the arrival of new ones. For six tense days, under the threat of nuclear war, the world watched and waited for a reply from the Soviet Union. Finally, on October 28, Soviet prime minister Nikita Khrushchev announced

Cuban exiles storm the beach during the Bay of Pigs invasion in April 1961. The U.S. Central Intelligence Agency (CIA) sponsored the unsuccessful attack, which led to the death or capture of all 1,400 soldiers. Visit www.vgsbooks.com for links to learn more about the Bay of Pigs invasion and the Cuban missile crisis.

that his country would meet U.S. demands in return for a promise that the United States would not invade Cuba. The Cuban missile crisis had ended, but not without damage to the relationships among all three nations.

Postrevolutionary Cuba

The first decade of revolutionary government in Cuba was marked by disorganization, inconsistencies, and trial and error. Castro and his lieutenants tried to put into practice their ideas about reforming agricultural industries and land ownership policies. In the early years of the U.S. trade embargo, many Cubans nearly starved. Because so much of the land in Cuba was used for sugarcane, farmers were unable to grow enough food to feed the population.

Castro ruled as a dictator, cracking down on any opposition to his regime. In the 1960s, Cubans who did not support the government, including writers, artists, and intellectuals, were targeted as "socially unacceptable" or as "dissidents" (people who disagreed with the political system). Thousands of people were jailed as political prisoners or went into exile. People were not allowed to speak out against or criticize the government, and freedom of expression was restricted. Trade unions (organized groups of workers) were disbanded, and the government took control of the media. Public displays of religion were banned, since religious belief was seen as antirevolutionary.

Over the years, Castro's emigration policy changed several times. Before 1961 it was fairly easy for people to leave Cuba for the United States. But in 1961, getting an exit visa (permission from the government to leave Cuba) became much more difficult. In the mid-1960s, as tensions between Cuba and the United States eased, Castro decided to allow another wave of emigration. Thousands of Cubans flew from Havana to Miami, Florida, in government-approved "freedom flights." By 1971, however, the flow of emigrants slowed down, and Castro stopped all freedom flights in 1973.

As the Cuban leadership gained more experience, conditions improved in the 1970s. Greatly assisted by financial aid from the Soviet Union—as well as by a newly trained workforce to replace the one that had left Cuba during the revolution—the nation gradually began to rebuild itself. The Castro regime worked tirelessly on two of the main cornerstones of the revolution: health care and education. Cuba drafted a new constitution in 1976, and Fidel Castro assumed the role of president, a position he has held ever since.

Economic and social problems in Cuba led to increasing numbers of public protests, however. In 1980 Castro announced that people who wanted to leave Cuba and emigrate to the United States were free

In 2003 these Cubans tried to reach the United States by sailing across the ocean on this **makeshift "boat,"** or *balsa*, made from a 1951 Chevy truck. They were returned to Cuba by the U.S. Coast Guard.

to do so. Over the course of five months, about 125,000 people left Cuba by boat and traveled to Miami, where a large community of Cuban exiles lives.

The collapse of the Soviet Union in 1991 had a devastating effect on Cuba's economy. In 1990 Castro put into place a policy called the Special Period in Peacetime, in which food and other goods were rationed (made available on a limited basis) and energy consumption was reduced. The economic crisis worsened until 1994, when signs of improvement appeared. The government began to encourage foreign investment in Cuba and to allow some private ownership of businesses. Tourism thrived, as visitors from Canada, Mexico, and Europe took advantage of the relaxed mood.

BALSEROS

Each year many Cubans try to sail from Cuba to the United States in small boats, inner tubes, and homemade rafts, called *balsas*. Those who flee Cuba in this way are known as *balseros*, or "rafters." The most creative "boat" was a 1951 Chevy truck, which was intercepted by the U.S. Coast Guard in July 2003. The vehicle had a pontoon made of 55-gallon oil drums and a propeller at the end of its drive shaft.

Another turning point came in January 1998, when Castro permitted Catholic leader Pope John Paul II to speak in Cuba. The people of Cuba welcomed the pope with a great outpouring of warmth, and hundreds of thousands of Cubans flocked to his outdoor services. The pope made a plea for human rights and religious freedom in Cuba and asked Castro to free political prisoners. Two hundred prisoners, including many who were being held on political charges, were released. Since the pope's visit, the Cuban government has allowed people to practice their religion more openly, but human rights abuses continue in Cuba. Dozens of prominent writers and journalists have been jailed in the early twenty-first century for criticizing the government.

Cuban soldiers guard an airplane after an attempted hijacking on April 1, 2003. Forty-six passengers were held hostage overnight by the hijackers.

In 2003 a number of Cubans tried to escape to Florida by hijacking airplanes or ferries. In March that year, six Cubans hijacked a Cuban plane from the Isle of Youth and flew to Key West, Florida. About half the passengers and crew chose to remain in the United States. In April eight Cuban hijackers commandeered a ferry with fifty passengers aboard, but they had to return to port in Mariel because they ran out of fuel. The Cuban military stormed the ferry, freeing the passengers and arresting the hijackers. Three hijackers were executed.

On the international front, Castro remains set against the United States and has alienated some of his former allies. In 2002 he offended Mexican president Vicente Fox, even calling him a liar. Tensions have slowly eased, however.

Government

Under the current constitution, Cuba's 609-member National Assembly of People's Power is elected every five years. All citizens over sixteen years of age are allowed to vote by secret ballot. Half the candidates for the assembly are nominated by members of public organizations, while the other half are chosen by municipal assemblies (similar to city councils).

Cuba has only one political party, the Cuban Communist Party, or PCC (Partido Comunista de Cuba), and all candidates for political office must be approved by the PCC. Opposition to the political system is discouraged, and anyone who criticizes the regime or attempts to organize opposition to it faces arrest.

The National Assembly elects the thirty-one-member Council of State, headed by the president, first vice president, five other vice presidents, and a secretary. The president nominates another body, the forty-four-member Council of Ministers, that runs affairs of state. The National Assembly meets twice a year to approve the Council of Ministers' decisions.

Fidel Castro *(left)* **and Jimmy Carter** *(right)* **shake hands during Carter's visit to Cuba in 2002.**

THE VARELA PROJECT

In 2002 more than eleven thousand Cubans signed a petition calling for free elections and freedom of expression. The petition, called the Varela Project, was applauded by former U.S. president Jimmy Carter when he visited Cuba in May 2002. Feeling threatened, Castro called for a constitutional amendment that would declare the principles of the People's Revolution "untouchable," effectively killing the Varela Project. The National Assembly approved the suggested amendment without debate in June 2003. In October the European Parliament awarded the 2002 Sakharov Award for Human Rights and Freedom of Thought to Osvaldo Payá, organizer of the Varela Project. Since then, signatures on the petition have doubled.

The president is both the chief of state and head of the government, serving as president of the Council of State and the Council of Ministers. Although the president is elected by the National Assembly, Castro has been the only candidate for the office.

Cuba is divided into fourteen provinces and one special municipality (Havana). Delegates to provincial assemblies are elected in the same way National Assembly delegates are elected. Delegates to the 169 municipal (city) assemblies are elected in their districts.

The People's Supreme Court is the highest judicial body in Cuba, with four chambers that deal with criminal, civil, military, and state security cases. All lawyers and judges are government employees.

THE PEOPLE

With a population of 11,272,600, Cuba is the most populous Caribbean island. Cuba's population has remained fairly stable, with an annual growth rate of just 0.4 percent. Population growth has been limited in part due to the mass emigration of Cubans to the United States since the revolution. Half a million Cubans left during the first decade alone, with a further 125,000 in 1980. The United States still accepts, on average, 20,000 Cuban immigrants each year.

◯ Ethnic Groups

In Cuba's history, the main ethnic groups were indigenous groups, Spanish, African, and Chinese. But as a result of intermarriage, most twenty-first-century Cubans are of mixed ethnic heritage.

In Cuba's early years as a Spanish colony, people with mixed Spanish and Indian heritage were known as mestizos. Mestizos in turn intermarried with other ethnic groups, and no purely indigenous people are left in Cuba. People of mixed Spanish and African background account

for a little more than half of the population, while 37 percent of the population is white, 11 percent is black, and 1 percent is Chinese.

The diversity of the Cuban people is reflected in many combinations of skin, eye, and hair color. Cubans group themselves in such categories as *leche con una gota de café* (milk with a drop of coffee), *café con leche* (coffee with milk), *negros de pasas* (black with kinky hair), *negros de pelo* (black with straight hair), *blanco* (white with light hair and eyes), *and blanquito* (white with dark hair and eyes).

Although the black population faced widespread discrimination before the revolution, since then Cuban society has followed the "melting pot" model. People see themselves primarily as Cubans and are less concerned with ethnicity.

Standard of Living

Three-quarters of Cubans are urban dwellers, with a full 19 percent living in Havana. Urban congestion creates problems such as pollution

RATION BOOKS

Starting in 1962, every Cuban family was issued a ration book, or *libreta*, to ensure that all citizens would receive a basic amount of food. With the book, which is stamped each time a purchase is made, a family is entitled to a standard ration every month, including rice, beans, oil, sugar, tomato sauce, soup, bread, coffee, cigars, and other necessities. A number of other items, such as soap and detergent, are distributed less frequently. Scarce items such as meat, chicken, fish, eggs, vegetables, and fruit are distributed when available. Children under seven years old and pregnant women receive regular milk rations. Residents of Havana receive a few more rations because it is harder for them to get fresh produce, meats, and fish, which are more readily available in rural areas. Rations are distributed at special stores called bodegas and cost very little.

and shortages of housing, food, and water. Because of the acute housing shortage, since 1998 Cubans who want to relocate to Havana have to show proof of prearranged housing and employment and receive official permission to move.

For the majority of Cubans, the standard of living has improved greatly since the revolution. Improvements in housing and health care have resulted in better living conditions and freedom from many diseases that were caused by poor sanitation in the past. Yet, because Cuba is not allowed to trade freely with other nations, and because its few resources have to be divided among all citizens, the standard of living remains lower than for most North Americans.

Cubans earn, on average, 200 pesos per month, or about $10. This wage needs to cover the cost of housing, electricity, telephone, transportation, and food bought from government-run stores. Cuba's state-sponsored food rationing system falls short of its goal of providing adequate nutrition for all citizens. A basic low-cost monthly ration—which includes rice, beans, eggs, coffee, ground beef, and bread—provides only enough food to last one week to ten days.

A clerk at a bodega marks off purchases in a customer's **ration book.**

Merchants sell jewelry and other handmade crafts to tourists at markets such as this one. The tourist industry helps Cubans earn U.S. dollars, which can be used at "dollar stores."

People who can afford it supplement these meager rations by buying food from farmers' markets.

Many items, such as clothing, toiletries, and household appliances, are not available or are available only in limited quantities at the government stores. These goods may be purchased at "dollar stores," privately owned shops that are licensed by the government and accept only U.S. dollars. People who work in the tourism industry, including employees of tour operations, hotels, restaurants, and bars, are able to earn U.S. dollars through tips. Other people get U.S. dollars from relatives living in the United States.

◔ Health and Social Services

Improved health care was one of the cornerstones of the People's Revolution, and the Castro regime has worked hard to meet that goal. Indeed, Cuba's health care system is the most advanced in Latin America.

Average life expectancy has risen from 55 years in 1959 to 76 years in the early twenty-first century. (On average, men in Cuba live to age 74 and women to age 78.) The infant mortality rate, which is the number of infant deaths per 1,000 live births, dropped from 60 in 1959 to 7.5 in the early twenty-first century, one of the lowest rates in the world. However, malnutrition is a serious problem in Cuba. At least 13 percent of the population, including many children, is undernourished.

Immediately following the revolution, Cuba faced serious shortages of medical workers because many of them had left the country. Within a decade, thousands of doctors and nurses were trained to fill the void, and that level of training has continued. After graduating from medical school, new doctors in Cuba must spend two years working in rural areas. More than fourteen thousand medical clinics, known as doctor houses, are scattered throughout the country. All health care is free for Cuban citizens, and waiting periods for treatment are short. The only health category that isn't free is medications, for which Cubans pay a small fee.

Cuba has had far greater success in controlling human immunodeficiency virus (HIV) and acquired immunodeficiency syndrome (AIDS) than any other developing nation, and it has one of the lowest HIV infection rates in the world. Starting in the early years of the epidemic, people with the disease have been quarantined (isolated) in sanatoriums, medical facilities where they receive treatment and care. However, the disease is becoming more common, largely due to the rapid growth in the number of tourists bringing the disease to the island.

One shortfall of Cuba's health care system is a chronic shortage of medicines and equipment, due to the U.S. embargo. This challenge has forced the nation to develop its own pharmaceutical (drug manufacturing) industry. Important strides are also being made in biotechnology, biomedical engineering, genetics, and other medical research.

Travel to Cuba is restricted for people from the United States. One exception is for visitors on humanitarian missions. These travelers often bring over-the-counter and **prescription drugs for Cuba's pharmacies** when they go.

Young children play at the **José Martí Day Care Center** in Batabanó, Cuba. The Cuban government provides affordable day care for working families.

Family planning is encouraged in Cuba, and most married couples limit their families to one or two children. Abortion is legal and free and is used as a method of reducing teenage pregnancies, which account for 14 percent of all pregnancies in Cuba.

Pregnant women can leave their jobs between their seventh and ninth month of pregnancy, and they receive up to one year of paid maternity leave. Fathers do not receive paternity leave. An excellent day care system operates throughout Cuba, priced according to family income. This service is essential for working women, since women constitute 42 percent of the workforce in Cuba.

For Cuban women who work and for men who have labor-intensive jobs such as mining, the official retirement age is fifty-five. For all other men, retirement occurs at the age of sixty. All retirees receive a pension (retirement income) based on their length of service. People who wish to continue working beyond retirement age receive supplemental income in addition to their salary.

The Cuban government provides housing for all citizens, based on a space allotment of 108 square feet (10 sq. m) per person. Families are required to pay rent (no more than 10 percent of family income) for a number of years, at which point they own the dwelling. People are not allowed to sell their apartments or houses, but they may trade with others.

Visit www.vgsbooks.com for links to websites with additional information about life in Cuba, including population statistics and more.

High school students gather for an exam. **Education in Cuba** is free for all students from elementary school through college.

Education

Education reform was another important aim of the Cuban revolution. While still a student in law school, Castro was dismayed by the inadequacy and inefficiency of Cuba's educational system. In prerevolutionary Cuba, only half of children aged 6 to 12 attended school. Castro vowed to make education accessible to all Cubans, and he kept his promise. In 1961 educational institutions were closed for a year, and teachers, professors, and high school and university students were sent throughout the country to teach people to read and write. Since Castro took power, Cuba's literacy rate has climbed from 75 percent to 97 percent, meaning that almost all Cuban citizens can read and write.

Military service is required for every Cuban male at the age of eighteen. Men who don't go to college spend three years in the service, while university students serve for one year. Men can also choose to spend this time working on a collective farm rather than joining the armed forces.

Following the revolution, all private schools were nationalized. Since then, education has been free, from elementary school through college. All Cuban children are required to attend school through grade twelve. Secondary school students also spend time working on farms. In rural schools, students spend half a day in the classroom and the other half on a farm. In urban schools, students spend a full month each year on farms. This helps the government pay for free education. It also gives students an understanding of the agricultural industry.

Following secondary school, students may choose to continue their education in technical schools or universities. Approximately 25 percent of secondary school students go on to attend universities. University students receive free accommodations, with breakfast and dinner provided. They also receive a small allowance, which increases slightly each school year. All degree programs are five years long, followed by a two-year period of required social service, when graduates work in their field of expertise for a small stipend (payment). After this they are free to find any job.

Cuba extends the benefits of its educational system to other developing nations. The name of the Isle of Youth stems from the educational program that takes place on the island. Special elementary and secondary schools, funded by the Cuban government, teach hundreds of students from developing nations. A similar training program is offered in Cuba's medical schools for students from Latin American and African nations, including Ethiopia, Mozambique, and Nicaragua.

COMMUNITY SERVICE

Every Cuban citizen is expected to do a certain amount of unpaid volunteer work. In exchange for the free services they receive from the government, people help out in the community by cleaning and maintaining public spaces, helping those who are unable to shop for themselves, and doing other chores.

Cuban high school students work in a field to fulfill their volunteer requirement.

CULTURAL LIFE

Cuban people are known for their love of life. They nurture their relationships with family, friends, neighbors, and coworkers. Regardless of education, social, or economic status, Cubans enjoy spending time with others, savoring music, sports, and festivals. The arts are accessible to all Cubans, thanks to financial support from the government.

Family life is the foundation of Cuban society. Many people, especially in rural areas, live in extended families that include grandparents and sometimes aunts and uncles. Since most women work outside the home, having grandparents or other relatives in the home is a great advantage. Older people with no families are cared for in homes for the elderly.

Religion

With its Spanish roots, Cuba has been a largely Roman Catholic country since the colonial era. In the 1960s, however, the revolutionary government discouraged organized religion by banning religious

publications and public processions. A constitutional amendment in 1992 restored freedom of religion, and since the pope's visit in 1998, more Cubans are attending religious services. There are also fifty-four Protestant (non-Catholic Christian) denominations in Cuba, the most popular being the Baptist faith.

Several Afro-Cuban religions are practiced in Cuba, a legacy of the large West African slave population that arrived from the 1500s to the 1700s. The most popular of these religions is Santeria, which originated with the Yoruba people of Nigeria. A combination of Roman Catholicism and the Yoruba faith, Santeria grew out of the Yoruba people's need to hide their religion. Because Yoruba slaves were not permitted to practice their religion in Cuba, they disguised their gods and goddesses, called orishas, in the identities of Roman Catholic saints. Although Catholic saints are considered to have attained perfection in heaven, orishas are imperfect beings like humans. Santeria followers also worship the spirits of their departed ancestors.

Some of the most important orishas are the creator god, Obatalá, who is associated with Jesus Christ and is always dressed in white; Obatalá's wife, Obudúa, goddess of the underworld, associated with the Virgin Mary; Obatalá's son, Elegguá, god of destiny, associated with Saint Anthony; and Ochún or Oshun, the goddess of love, who wears yellow, loves honey, and is associated with the Virgin del Cobre, the patron saint of Cuba. There are an estimated four thousand Santeria priests in Cuba, many of whom still speak the Yoruba language.

◉ Holidays and Festivals

Like many of their Caribbean neighbors, Cubans love to party—and that's what happens during festivals and holidays. Carnival is the most important festival in Cuba. It originated in the 1700s as a time for African slaves to celebrate the end of the sugar harvest. The most spectacular Carnival celebration takes place in Santiago de Cuba, the center of Afro-Cuban culture. During the last two weeks of July, the city is abuzz, and drums reign supreme as costumed people crowd the bars and take to the streets to celebrate with music, dance, and song. All major cities in Cuba have their own Carnival celebrations, but at different times of the year. Havana's Carnival takes place during the last two weeks of February.

Other festivals, such as the Havana International Jazz Festival in February, the International Guitar Festival in May, and the Havana Festival of Contemporary Music in October, revolve around Cuban music, which plays a large role in people's lives.

Most of Cuba's major holidays commemorate political events. The most important of these is National Rebellion Day, which remembers Castro's attack on the army barracks in Santiago de Cuba on July 26, 1953, with a three-day holiday from July 25 through July 27. Other holidays include Liberation Day (January 1), which marks the people's liberation from the Batista regime in 1959, and Day of Cuban Culture (October 10), marking the beginning of the First War of Independence in 1868. The only nonpolitical holiday is Christmas (December 25).

Cubans have only recently begun celebrating Christmas again. In 1969 the holiday was officially dropped. Christmas trees and nativity scenes were banned, except in tourist venues such as hotels. In 1997 Castro reinstated Christmas as a public holiday. Thousands of Cuban Christians attend church services on Christmas Eve, and bells ring out across the land at midnight. People decorate their homes, party with friends and family, and prepare a special meal of pork, beans, fruit, and apple cider.

Literature

The earliest literary works in Cuba were written in the language of the conquistadores, Spanish, which is the nation's official language. Much of Cuba's literature reflects the ongoing struggle of its people for freedom—from Spanish rulers, from slave owners, from rich U.S. business owners, and from Cuban dictators. The most famous literary figure of the colonial era was José Martí (1853–1895), who started the Second War of Independence. Martí's collected poems, essays, and plays fill twenty-five volumes.

José Martí

Twentieth-century poet Nicolás Guillén (1902–1989) challenged racial and social inequalities. After spending years in exile during Batista's rule, Guillén returned to Cuba in 1961 and wrote poetry celebrating the revolution. Alejo Carpentier (1904–1980), considered Cuba's greatest novelist, also spent most of the years between 1927 and 1959 in exile and returned to Cuba following the revolution. *Concierto Barroco* (1974) is considered Carpentier's most significant novel. In 1992 poet Dulce María Loynaz (1902–1997) won the Miguel de Cervantes Award, the most important literary award in the Spanish-speaking world.

ERNEST HEMINGWAY

Nobel Prize-winning American author Ernest Hemingway (1899–1961) made his home in Cuba for twenty years before moving back to the United States in 1959. Cubans affectionately referred to him as Papa Hemingway. His home near Havana is maintained as a museum *(above)*. Hemingway's 1952 novel *The Old Man and the Sea* was set in Cuba and won the Pulitzer Prize. Visit www.vgsbooks.com for links to websites with information about the life and writings of Ernest Hemingway.

The People's Revolution had a significant impact on the literary arts in Cuba. As more Cubans gained access to higher education, an increasing number of people became interested in reading and the study of literature. Noteworthy contemporary literary figures include novelists Edmundo Desnoes, Georgina Herrera, Nancy Morejón, and Leonardo Padura Fuentes. Cuba's most widely recognized black poet is Heberto Padilla, who has served prison time for his antirevolutionary writing.

Self-exiled Cuban writers who continue to write in Spanish include Hilda Perera, Guillermo Cabrera Infante, and Antonio Benítez Rojo. Cristina García is a Cuban American who emigrated to the United States when she was only two years old. She writes about her land of birth as well as about Cubans who live in the United States.

◉ Music and Dance

Music has long fueled the spirits of the Cuban people in their struggles. From the early African slaves to the impoverished prerevolution campesinos (laborers), Cubans have used music and song to boost morale and celebrate triumphs. Cuba's legacy to the world of music has been huge. The strains of rumba, mambo, salsa, and Cuban jazz all have roots in the Afro-Cuban *son* rhythms that originated in the hills of Oriente province more than two hundred years ago. The instruments used to play this native Cuban music are guitar, *tres* (a small Cuban guitar with three pairs of strings), bass, claves (two sticks used to tap out the beat), bongo drums, trumpet, and guiro (a

A Cuban street band in Santiago de Cuba attracts dancers from the crowd. Music is a big part of Cuban life.

gourd from the *güira* fruit that is rubbed with a stick). A variety of African drums and Spanish guitars show up in all Cuban music forms. Over the years, these instruments have been joined by various brass and wind instruments, such as the saxophone and trumpet.

Music and song continue to play a central role in the lives of modern Cubans, and groups of musicians may be found entertaining passersby on city streets any time of day or night. High-quality recordings of Cuban singers and musical groups are produced by a government-owned recording studio and are available throughout Cuba at reasonable prices. Popular contemporary musicians and groups include Los Van Van, Sierra Maestra, Eliades Ochoa, Cuarteto Patria, Los Muñequitos de Matanzas, Clave y Guaguancó, Irakere, as well as singers Silvio Rodríguez, Celina González, and Lázaro Ros.

One of Cuba's most important contemporary music stars is Juan de Marcos González. He has devoted the last twenty-five years of his life to promoting Cuban music among young Cubans as well as exporting it to the rest of the world. He was a central figure in organizing the Buena Vista Social Club and the Afro-Cuban Allstars, groups that showcase multigenerational Cuban musical talents.

Visit www.vgsbooks.com for links to websites with additional information about Cuba's interesting and lively culture. Learn about Cuba's art, music, and literature, as well as the strong influence Cuba's African heritage has had on the country's culture.

Cuban dance, much like the music, bears a rich African legacy and has grown popular throughout the world. Many of the dance forms, which include the rumba, mambo, cha-cha-cha, and salsa, grew from the music of the same name. The rumba originated in African slave dances, then evolved into the mambo and the more simplified cha-cha-cha of the twentieth century. A dance developed by Cubans of Spanish ancestry was the habanera, which later gave rise to the Argentine tango and the Cuban bolero.

The Russian influence in Cuba after the revolution gave rise to a ballet tradition. The National Ballet of Cuba has received international acclaim over the past half century, thanks in large part to Alicia Alonso, Latin America's most famous ballerina.

Alicia Alonso

Visual Arts

Archaeological findings from the pre-Columbian societies of Cuba have shown that the native people were artistic. They carved designs into their tools and vessels, crafted jewelry from stone and bone, and wove feathers and reeds. The best examples of pre-Columbian art were discovered in a cave on the Isle of Youth in 1910. The cave walls and ceilings are covered with more than two hundred paintings.

After the arrival of the Spanish, Cuban art was influenced by European painting styles. Following Cuban independence in the early twentieth century, many of the country's visual artists studied in Europe. A new style of Cuban art was influenced by artists such as Paul Gauguin and Pablo Picasso.

Since the revolution, a style known as naive art has flourished. Created by artists with no formal training, this folk art uses bright colors and bold strokes to depict Cuba's

A wall covered in colorful **mosaic tiles** shows off the Cuban naive style of art. This wall in Havana is just a portion of a mosaic house that artists have completely covered with bits of ceramic tile.

vivid urban and rural landscapes, as well as humorous interpretations of Cuban society. Thousands of works of this style are sold throughout Cuba and are very much in demand by tourists.

Poster art in Cuba gained much respect since its use as a medium of mass communication beginning in the 1960s. Since then graphic art has spread to billboards that dot the countryside and murals that adorn walls of buildings with keen political and social commentaries.

Architecture

Cuba's architecture reflects different periods in the country's history, creating a vivid collage of European, American, Russian, and Cuban design styles. The oldest architectural style in Cuba is found in rural areas, in the thatched-roof peasants' dwellings known as bohíos. Colonial buildings date back to the 1500s. These include the home of Cuba's colonizer, Diego Velázquez, which was built in 1522 and is the oldest house on the island. The Iglesia de San Juan Bautista, in the small town of Remedios, dates from 1545 and is one of the finest churches in Cuba. In Havana the Real Fuerza, built between 1558 and 1577, is the oldest colonial castle in the Americas.

Many buildings in Cuba were erected during the seventeenth and eighteenth centuries and are characterized by ornate baroque decoration. Among these are several magnificent churches, such as the Catedral de San Cristóbal de la Habana in Havana and the Iglesia de Nuestra Señora de la Soledad in Camagüey. Elegant palaces built

The Catedral de San Cristóbal de la Habana in La Habana Vieja is a prime example of the early baroque architecture of Cuba. The plaza in front of the cathedral is a popular meeting spot.

during this period include the Palacio de los Capitanes Generales and the Palacio del Segundo Cabo, both in Havana.

Most of the nineteenth-century architecture in Cuba was built in the neoclassical style, which drew inspiration from classical Greek and Roman forms. Among the many public buildings constructed during this period were grand theaters such as the Teatro Principal in Camagüey, Teatro Sauto in Matanzas, and Teatro Tomás Terry in Cienfuegos.

U.S. and Russian influences are seen in the modern designs of private homes, office buildings, apartment buildings, and factories that were built during the twentieth century. Since the revolution in 1959, a uniquely Cuban style of architecture has emerged that mirrors the open, airy Caribbean climate and culture. The Palacio de las Convenciones and the Estadio Panamericano in Havana and the Antonio Maceo Airport and Teatro José María Heredia in Santiago de Cuba are examples.

Sports

Cuba has no professional athletes or sports teams. But from the early days of the revolution, the government has funded sports facilities and organizations and has encouraged Cubans, especially students, to participate in amateur sports. Physical education and sports are an integral part of the school system and community life. In 1961 the National Sports Institute was founded to provide free or low-cost access to sports facilities and events to all Cubans.

Baseball, or *béisbol*, is Cuba's national sport and has been played there since the 1870s. The Taino are believed to have played a similar game, called *batos*, before the arrival of the Spanish. The Cuban national baseball team, the Cuban All-Stars, is the best in Latin America and won an Olympic gold medal in 1996. Other sports Cubans enjoy include basketball, soccer, tennis, swimming, rowing, and sailing.

Cuba is a world leader in amateur boxing and has won several Olympic gold medals in the sport. The nation has also won Olympic gold medals in volleyball, wrestling, and judo. In 1991 Cuba hosted the Pan American Games and placed first overall, winning 140 medals and becoming the first Latin American country to beat the United States. (The Pan American Games, held every four years in the year before the

Watching television is a popular activity in Cuba, and 80 percent of Cubans own their own TV. The two major channels are Cuba Visión and Tele Rebelde, which offer educational programming, social and political commentary, news, sports, soap operas, and films. Hotels carry CNN, but it is not available to Cuban citizens.

Members of the **Cuban All-Stars baseball team** pose with their gold medals after defeating the United States in the 2003 Pan American Games held in the Dominican Republic.

Olympics, bring together athletes from the countries of the Americas to compete in amateur sports, similar to the Olympic Games.) Cuba placed fifth overall at the 1992 Olympics and ninth at both the 1996 and the 2000 Olympics.

Food

Cuban food has been influenced mostly by Spanish cuisine, with African touches as well. The flavoring of favorite dishes comes from onions, garlic, tomatoes, limes, oranges, and mild spices such as cumin and oregano. Cubans love meat. Pork and chicken are eaten most often, since beef and lamb are not as readily available. Fish and seafood, including tuna, hake, red snapper, shrimp, and lobster, are very much in demand when available. A fast-growing fish species called tilapia is being raised on fish farms to meet the large demand.

Rice has traditionally been the staple starch in Cuba. But since the Special Period in Peacetime that began in 1990, Cubans have been growing and eating more root vegetables—boniato (sweet potato), yucca, and *malanga*—because they are easier to grow than rice. Other

---

MOROS Y CRISTIANOS

Moros y cristianos (Moors and Christians) is a Cuban staple dish of black beans and rice. The black beans represent the Moors, or Muslim Arabs who invaded Spain centuries ago, and the white rice represents Spanish Christians.

1 tablespoon olive oil

1 medium red onion, finely chopped

1 small red pepper, finely chopped

2 cloves garlic, minced

1½ teaspoons chili powder

¼ teaspoon cayenne pepper

1 14.5-ounce can diced tomatoes

1½ cups cooked black beans

salt and pepper to taste

2 to 3 cups cooked white rice

¼ cup chopped scallions (for garnish)

1. Heat the olive oil in a large skillet over medium heat.
2. Add the onion, red pepper, and garlic. Turn heat down, cover, and cook until softened, about 7 minutes.
3. Stir in remaining ingredients, except rice. Cover and simmer for 10 to 20 minutes, or until heated through.
4. Serve over hot, cooked rice, and garnish with scallions.

A festive-looking dish of **red beans and rice** *(top)* and tasty **fried yucca** *(bottom)* are

commonly eaten foods are beans, corn, potatoes, plantains, and cabbage. Cubans also enjoy many types of tropical fruit, including mangoes, papayas, bananas, pineapples, oranges, and grapefruit.

Typical Cuban dishes consist of meat or fish, such as roast pork, roast suckling pig, or fried chicken, accompanied by rice, beans, and a boiled vegetable such as yucca or malanga, or *tostones* (fried plantains). But many people cannot afford to eat meat very often, so they make do with rice, beans, and vegetables. The most popular dessert in Cuba is ice cream, called *helado*.

THE ECONOMY

Maintaining a healthy economy has been the primary challenge for postrevolutionary Cuba. Lower sugar and nickel prices on the world market and increases in petroleum costs have placed stress on the Cuban economy, as has the U.S. embargo on trade with Cuba. Castro's attempts to stifle economic competition also create problems. With low salaries and lack of opportunities for advancement, many employees lack motivation to be productive.

Cuba's dependence on the Soviet Union for support in keeping the economy afloat came to an abrupt end in 1991 when the Soviet Union collapsed. Searching for new ways to stimulate the Cuban economy, Castro decided to permit joint ventures between foreign investors and the Cuban government. Cuba has entered into several successful arrangements with foreign companies, but the Cuban government holds the majority of company shares, or ownership, in these businesses. Joint ventures include nickel mining operations with Canadian companies and tourist resorts with German and French companies.

The Cuban government has also taken steps toward greater acceptance of private businesses. For example, Cubans who own plots of land can grow fruit and vegetables that they can then sell to other Cubans. In the early twenty-first century, 65,000 of these small private farms existed, and together they produced more food than all of Cuba's state-run farms combined. In November 2002, the National Assembly voted to allow private farmers to keep 70 percent of their profits, while the rest goes to the government. Previously, farmers had to give the government an equal or larger share of profits than they kept for themselves.

An important but unofficial contribution to the Cuban economy is money sent to relatives and friends by Cubans living abroad. Most of these payments, called remittances, come from families in the United States. Remittances contribute between $800 million and $1 billion per year to the Cuban economy and provide many Cubans with access to U.S. dollars.

Tourism

Services contribute about 58 percent of Cuba's gross domestic product (GDP), and about half of all Cuban workers are employed in the service sector. Tourism has become the most important service industry in Cuba, contributing more than $2 billion to the economy annually. Following the revolution, tourism had dropped off greatly, primarily because the United States banned its citizens from spending money in Cuba. As regulations on investment in Cuba were eased in the early 1990s, foreign and Cuban citizens began redeveloping the tourism industry. Canadian investors were among the first to get involved, and Canadians have become Cuba's largest group of visitors. The European countries of Germany, Italy, Spain, and France together contribute more than half of Cuba's tourists, while Mexicans are the most frequent Latin American visitors.

Although most tourist hotels are state owned, some of the more luxurious ones are managed by European or Canadian companies. The majority of small-business owners in Cuba work at enterprises that serve tourists, such as restaurants, bed-and-breakfasts, and craft outlets. Small restaurants called *paladares* are located in private homes. Many Cuban families, especially in small towns, free up one or two rooms in their homes to rent to tourists. These types of businesses are strictly controlled by the government so that they do not provide too much competition to state-run enterprises.

The blue sign above this door indicates that the **homeowners rent rooms** to tourists. For more information about travel to Cuba, see links available at www.vgsbooks.com.

Since the 1990s, the success of the tourism industry has begun to challenge the class-less society that Castro's government has worked so hard to promote. Workers in the tourism industry have access to U.S. dollars through tips and often earn more money than other Cubans do. Able to afford a better lifestyle, these workers are becoming a more privileged class.

An interesting development in the Cuban tourism industry is known as health tourism. Because of Cuba's advanced, low-cost health care system, many people, especially from Latin American countries, travel to Cuba to receive medical treatment. Cuba is also promoting ecotourism—touring or visiting natural habitats in a way that mimimizes the impact on the environment.

Sugar

After sugar was introduced to Cuba by Spanish colonists, sugar production sustained the Cuban economy almost single-handedly for centuries. But as sugar prices have fluctuated over the years, Cuba has found it increasingly difficult to rely solely on sugar to finance its imports and other expenses. Many of the sugar mills in the country are so old—dating from the 1800s—that the government has had to shut them down for renovations. It could be years before these mills are back in production.

About 400,000 Cubans work in the sugar industry. The sugarcane harvest, which used to take half a year when it was done by hand, was

Raw sugar pours off the back of a truck. The sugar industry has traditionally played a key role in the Cuban economy.

SUGARCANE

Sugarcane is a species of grass, which can grow over 8 feet (3 m) high. The flesh inside the cane, or stalk, is full of a sweet liquid. The cane is cut and taken to large factories, where the juice is pressed out and made into molasses, which is then crystalized into sugar. The sugar is refined, and the brown color is removed to produce a white sugar. Molasses can be reintroduced to make various shades of brown sugar. Molasses can also be fermented to produce rum. The remaining material from the cane is not wasted. It is used as fuel and to manufacture paper products, fiberboard, and animal feed.

mechanized following the revolution. However, fuel shortages since the early 1990s have caused some harvesters to go back to manual methods. This slows down the harvest, making the product more costly. Tourism revenues (income) have surpassed sugar exports, dropping sugar to second place in generating revenue for the nation.

◐ Mining

Nickel is Cuba's most important export after sugar. Since the early 1990s, Canadian companies have joined with the Cuban government to mine nickel. The mineral is then shipped to Canada for refining, and finally sold in Western Europe. Other important minerals that are mined in Cuba are cobalt, copper, chromite, tungsten, manganese, and iron ore.

Since the mid-1990s, Cuba has begun exploiting its crude oil reserves along the northern coastline. Since most of the crude oil extracted from these wells is very high in sulfur, it is unsuitable for use as an automotive fuel (to run cars and trucks), which needs to be far purer. Therefore, the oil is used primarily for generating electricity.

◐ Agriculture

One of most important actions undertaken by Castro's government was land reform. Before the revolution, nearly half of all farmable land was owned by just 1 percent of landowners. In 1959 an agrarian reform law nationalized all farms larger than 988 acres (400 hectares). In 1963 a second reform law followed, giving the government control over all land holdings larger than 160 acres (65 hectares). The land that was taken over was turned into state farms.

Since the early 1990s, when the government began allowing some private enterprise, more than half of the state-controlled land has been returned to the people who live and work on it. This land has been converted into cooperative farms, groupings of several small, private

A worker tends to a field of cabbages. **Cooperative farms** have helped farmers use supplies and sell goods more efficiently while also providing fresh produce at reasonable prices to shoppers.

farm plots that are managed as a single farm. In this way, the farmers are able to buy supplies in larger quantities and pay less for them because of discounts that go along with larger purchases. The cooperative arrangement also lets farmers get better prices for their products, because they have larger amounts to sell.

All sugarcane farms are still owned and operated by the government, but farmers with private plots are free to grow tobacco, coffee, grain, fruit, and vegetables. Growers have to sell their products to the government at prices set by the government. Anything over and above the production quota—the amount each farmer is expected to produce in a given time—may be sold to other Cubans or tourists.

The agriculture sector of Cuba's economy produces about 8 percent of the gross domestic product (GDP)—the total annual value of a country's products. The chief agricultural products are sugarcane, tobacco, citrus fruits, coffee, rice, potatoes, beans, and livestock. About 25 percent of the Cuban labor force works in agriculture.

Manufacturing

Next to sugar, petroleum is Cuba's most significant manufactured product. Next in importance are cigars and cigarettes. Cuba produces the world's finest cigars. The sandy soil in Pinar del Río province provides perfect conditions for growing superior-quality tobacco. All Cuban cigars are individually hand rolled, labeled, and boxed.

Cuba has been investing large sums of money in its pharmaceutical and medical technology industries. Apart from the urgent need for

Workers roll tobacco leaves into **handmade cigars.** Cuba is known throughout the world for its fine cigars.

Most of Cuba's tobacco crop is used to make the cigars that Cuba is famous for. The tobacco plants are carefully tended. When the plant is about 3 feet (1 m) high, the top leaves are picked off, strung up, and dried in a barn. Next, they are sprayed with water and fermented, then dried thoroughly before being shipped to a cigar factory.

these materials for domestic use, the country's leaders are also aware of their potential value as export products. More than two hundred Cuban pharmaceutical products are being marketed in developing nations, and foreign partners are testing other products to be sold throughout the world.

Other important manufactured items include chemicals, cement, mahogany lumber, agricultural machinery, textiles, shoes, food, and beverages. The industrial sector of the economy accounts for about 35 percent of GDP and employs 25 percent of the labor force.

◉ Foreign Trade

Before the revolution, 70 percent of Cuba's trade was conducted with the United States. But that came to an abrupt end in 1960 when Cuba seized and nationalized all foreign-owned land and businesses, including nearly 6,000 U.S. companies, worth an estimated $6 billion. In retaliation, the United States imposed a trade embargo, cutting off all imports and exports between Cuba and the United States. Cuba sought other trading partners and eventually built a very close relationship with the Soviet Union. By the time the Soviet Union collapsed in 1991, that nation was buying 81 percent of Cuba's exports while providing Cuba with 60 percent of its imports.

In the twenty-first century, Russia's trade with Cuba has declined to 13 percent of Cuba's exports and a very small percentage of its imports. Besides Russia, the major Cuban export partners are the Netherlands, Canada, Spain, and China. Cuba exports sugar, nickel, tobacco and cigars, fish, medical products, citrus fruits, rum, and coffee. Cuba imports goods and supplies from Venezuela, Mexico, Spain, France, Canada, China, and Italy. Primary imports include petroleum, food, chemicals, machinery, and equipment.

The Helms-Burton Act, passed in the United States in 1996, imposes trade sanctions (economic measures intended to punish a nation or force it to do something) against U.S. trading partners that trade with Cuba and penalizes them for investing in Cuban businesses. As a result, many countries are cautious about trading with Cuba for fear of suffering huge losses in revenues from trade with the United States. Yet, despite the embargo, it is now permissible for a few U.S. companies are exporting food to Cuba, primarily for use by the tourism industry.

Transportation

The transportation sector in Cuba has faced huge challenges since the breakdown of trading with the Soviet Union in the early 1990s, which led to a serious fuel shortage. Unable to purchase enough petroleum to

Commuters may ride in one of these *camellos*, or "camels," to get around Havana. The buses get their name from the two-humped design.

fuel its transportation needs, Cuba has had to limit bus and train service. Consequently, hitchhiking has become a regular method of travel for large numbers of Cubans. It is not unusual to see dozens of people waiting at highway intersections to hitch rides, and open-topped dump trucks filled with standing passengers.

In Cuba, license plates on vehicles are color coded to indicate differences in ownership. Yellow signifies private ownership, while state-owned vehicles have blue or brown plates. Military vehicles have green plates, diplomats have black plates, foreign residents have orange plates, and tourist rental cars have maroon plates.

The average Cuban cannot afford to own a car. The people who do often have vintage American cars from before the revolution—more than forty years old. A few Cubans own more recent models of Russian automobiles. Most people use bicycles to get around in urban areas and for short trips in rural areas. At the beginning of the fuel crisis in the early 1990s, the government gave bicycles to all Cubans who did not already have one.

Cuba has one of the best-developed networks of roads and highways in Latin America, with just under 18,530 miles (29,820 km) of paved highways. Cuba is the only Caribbean country with a functioning railway system. But the public rail service is under a great deal of strain due to aging equipment and tracks as well as major fuel shortages. Trains to many destinations are often canceled.

Modern cars are scarce in Cuba.

Fidel Castro *(left)* talks with his brother Raúl *(right)* during a meeting of the Cuban government. Raúl serves as first vice president (directly under Fidel) and minister of the Revolutionary Army. Despite his many injustices, Fidel Castro remains popular in Cuba because he ended homelessness and illiteracy.

The Future

Cuba in the twenty-first century presents a rare example of Communism in practice. The forty-plus years since the revolution have been shaped by two powerful forces: the U.S. trade embargo and Fidel Castro's steadfast anti-American stance. The embargo and other U.S. sanctions on Cuba have caused many hardships for Cuban citizens. Castro's stubborn determination has also caused many difficulties for his country.

During the early years of the revolution, Cubans who did not leave the country threw their wholehearted support behind their leader. They stood by Castro as he reformed the ailing public health, educational, agricultural, and industrial sectors. They cheered as his Communist policies spread the nation's resources among the people. But Cubans are no longer isolated from the rest of the world, and they see neighboring countries progressing economically while they remain at a standstill. Many Cubans are weary of waiting for improvements, while others see that progress brings new problems. Cubans are also impatient with the regime's repressive actions in punishing people who oppose Castro.

Meanwhile, Castro himself is getting older, with no official plans for a post-Castro Cuba. His designated successor, his brother Raúl, is only a little younger, leaving the Cuban people as well as the rest of the world wondering where the future leadership will come from. The people of Cuba hope that they will not lose the freedoms they have already won but will be able to build on them further into the twenty-first century.

CA. 3500 B.C. Cuba's first inhabitants settle the area.

A.D. 1250 The Taino people arrive in Cuba.

1492 Christopher Columbus lands in what he calls "the most beautiful land human eyes have ever seen."

1512 Diego Velázquez begins establishing the first Spanish settlements in Cuba.

1515 Santiago de Cuba becomes the capital of the new Spanish colony.

1522 African slaves are brought to Cuba.

1607 Havana becomes the new capital of Cuba.

1700 Tobacco gains importance as Cuba's primary export.

1728 The University of Havana is founded.

1762-1763 Great Britain takes control of Havana during the Seven Years' War and permits Cuba to trade with British American colonies.

1800 Sugar becomes Cuba's primary export.

1837 The first railroad in Latin America is built in Havana.

1839 Cirilo Villaverde writes the classic antislavery novel *Cecilia Valdés*.

1868-1878 Cuba's First War of Independence, also called the Ten Years' War, is fought.

1886 Slavery is abolished in Cuba.

1895-1898 José Martí leads a revolt against Spanish rule, starting the Second War of Independence.

1898 The United States declares war on Spain in April, starting the Spanish-American War. Spain surrenders in July.

1899-1902 A U.S. military government controls Cuba.

1902 Cuba gains independence under President Tomás Estrada Palma.

1934 Army sergeant Fulgencio Batista seizes power and rules for the next twenty-five years.

1948 Alicia Alonso establishes the Alicia Alonso Ballet Company, which later becomes the National Ballet of Cuba.

1953 Fidel Castro and a group of rebels attack the Moncada army barracks in Santiago de Cuba, hoping to spark a revolt. The effort fails, and the rebels are jailed.

1955 Castro is freed from prison and travels to Mexico.

1956   Castro and his band of rebels arrive in Oriente province.
        The twelve survivors set up a base of operations in the Sierra
        Maestra.

1959   Under pressure from the rebels, Batista flees, and Castro and his fol-
        lowers take control of Cuba.

1960   Castro nationalizes large companies, including many U.S. businesses.

1961   A group of Cuban exiles, backed by the United States, invade the Bay of Pigs in
        southwestern Cuba. Castro's army quickly defeats the invaders. The United
        States enacts a trade embargo against Cuba.

1962   In the Cuban missile crisis, the United States forces the Soviet Union to remove
        missiles from Cuba to reduce the threat of a nuclear war.

1974   Novelist Alejo Carpentier publishes *Concierto Barroco*.

1976   Boxer Teófilo Stevenson turns down an offer of $5 million to turn professional and
        fight world champion Muhammad Ali.

1980   Castro allows people to leave Cuba for the United States. About 125,000 Cubans sail to
        the United States.

1990   Castro declares a "Special Period in Peacetime," restricting food rations, energy use,
        and other expenses.

1991   The collapse of the Soviet Union leads to severe economic problems in Cuba, which relied
        on the Soviets for economic support.

1992   Poet Dulce María Loynaz wins the Miguel de Cervantes Award.

1994   Castro begins to allow foreign investment and limited private business in Cuba.

1996   The Helms-Burton Act is enacted in the United States, tightening the embargo against
        trade with Cuba. The Cuban All-Stars baseball team wins the gold medal at the
        Olympics in Atlanta, Georgia.

1998   Pope John Paul II visits Cuba, calling for religious freedom and an end to human
        rights abuses.

2003   Castro imprisons and executes dissidents trying to leave Cuba.

2004   Ties between Cuba and the United States worsen as U.S. president George W.
        Bush tightens U.S. restrictions on travel to and trade with Cuba and suspends
        immigration talks with Cuba.

COUNTRY NAME República de Cuba (Republic of Cuba)

AREA 44,218 square miles (114,524 sq. km)

MAIN LANDFORMS Isla de la Juventud (Isle of Youth), Sierra Maestra, Sierra del Escambray, Sierra de los Órganos, Sierra del Rosario, Ciénaga de Zapata

HIGHEST POINT Pico Turquino, 6,540 feet (1,993 m) above sea level

LOWEST POINT Sea level

MAJOR RIVERS Cauto, Sagua la Grande, Zaza

ANIMALS jutías (tree rats), bats, majas (boa constrictors), snakes, crocodiles, iguanas, lizards, salamanders, manatees, sea turtles

CAPITAL CITY Havana (La Habana)

OTHER MAJOR CITIES Santiago de Cuba, Camagüey, Holguín, Santa Clara, Cienfuegos

OFFICIAL LANGUAGE Spanish

MONETARY UNIT Peso, convertible peso, U.S. dollar. 100 centavos = 1 peso.

CURRENCY

Three types of currency are used in Cuba. The nation's original currency, the peso, is made up of 100 centavos. The currency is available in notes of 1, 3, 5, 10, 20, 50, and 100 pesos *(shown at right)*. Coins are available in 1 and 3 pesos, and 1, 2, 5, 20, and 40 centavos. Convertible pesos have the same value as U.S. dollars. They are available in 1, 3, 5, 10, 20, 50, and 100 peso notes, and coins of 1 peso, and 5, 10, 25, and 50 cents. The third type of currency is the U.S. dollar.

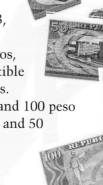

Currency **Fast Facts**

The Cuban flag is rectangular with three horizontal blue stripes alternating with two white stripes. On the left side of the flag is a solid red triangle with a five-pointed white star in the center. The flag was designed by Narciso López, a former Spanish general living in the United States. He used the flag during an unsuccessful attempt to join Cuba to the United States in 1850. The single white star on the red background and the horizontal blue and white stripes were patterned after the U.S. flag, with the idea that Cuba would become a U.S. state. The flag was officially adopted following Cuban independence in 1902.

The Cuban national anthem, *La Bayamesa* ("The Bayamo Song"), was composed in 1867–1868 by Pedro Figueredo as a battle cry to rally Cubans to the First War of Independence. Bayamo is located in the former province of Oriente, where the war started.

La Bayamesa
Hasten to battle, men of Bayamo,
For the homeland looks proudly to you.
You do not fear a glorious death,
Because to die for the country is to live.

To live in chains
Is to live in dishonor and ignominy.
Hear the clarion call,
Hasten, brave ones, to battle!

 For a link where you can listen to Cuba's national anthem, *La Bayamesa*, go to www.vgsbooks.com.

ALICIA ALONSO (b. 1921) Born in Havana, Alonso began studying dance in 1931. She made her professional debut as a ballet dancer in the United States in 1938 and became a member of the New York City Ballet in 1940. She danced as a prima ballerina in many countries. In 1948 she founded a dance company that became the National Ballet of Cuba, where she is still director and choreographer.

FULGENCIO BATISTA (1901–1973) Born in Oriente province, Batista joined the Cuban armed forces in 1921. He was a sergeant when he proclaimed himself general and seized power from the seated president in 1934. From then until 1940, he ruled from behind the scenes. Batista was elected president in 1940, but he lost the position in 1944. In 1952 he set himself up as a dictator, ruling the nation until he was routed by the People's Revolution in 1958. He lived in exile on the Portuguese island of Madeira and died in Madrid, Spain.

LYDIA CABRERA (1899–1991) Cabrera was born in Havana and went to Paris in 1927 to study. She became interested in Afro-Cuban culture and eventually wrote twenty-three books about the subject, including a dictionary of the Yoruba language. Her work about Santeria, *El Monte (The Mountain)*, is considered the most important book about the Afro-Cuban religion. Cabrera moved back to Cuba in 1938 but fled to Madrid and then to Miami after the People's Revolution in 1958.

MARÍA CARIDAD COLÓN (b. 1959) A native of Baracoa, in eastern Cuba, Caridad Colón began competing in track and field events as a teenager. She became the first Latin American woman to win an Olympic gold medal when she won the javelin competition at the 1980 Olympics in Moscow. She went on to work for the Cuban Ministry of Sports.

FIDEL CASTRO (b. 1926) The leader of the People's Revolution and of Cuba ever since, Castro was born in Oriente province and was educated in private schools. He earned a law degree from the University of Havana. In 1953 Castro led an unsuccessful attack against President Batista and was imprisoned. Pardoned in 1955, he exiled himself to Mexico, where he planned his second assault on the Batista regime. Following the revolution, Castro became prime minister in 1959. Since 1976 he has been president, with dictatorial power.

CAMILO CIENFUEGOS (1932–1959) Born in Havana, Cienfuegos was forced to cut short his education in art school because of financial difficulties. He was appointed chief of staff of the armed forces in the new regime, but shortly afterward his plane was lost over the ocean. Some Cubans believe that Castro had Cienfuegos killed.

ELIÁN GONZÁLEZ (b. 1993) In November 1999, six-year-old González—a native of Cárdenas, Cuba—became an international celebrity when he was found clinging to an inner tube off Florida's coast. His mother had died as she attempted to escape with the boy to Florida. In June 2000, the U.S. Department of Justice ruled that González should be returned to his father in Cuba. He was reuinted with his family in Cuba on June 28, 2000.

JUAN DE MARCOS GONZÁLEZ (b. 1954) González grew up in a musical family in Havana. After earning a Ph.D. in engineering, he worked in Cuba's Agronomic Science Institute. While still in school, González cofounded a musical group called Sierra Maestra. The group's phenomenal success made Cuban music popular around the world. González has gone on to form other Cuban musical groups, such as the Buena Vista Social Club and the Afro-Cuban Allstars.

SALVADOR GONZÁLEZ ESCALONA (b. 1948) Contemporary artist González Escalona converted a section of the Callejón de Hamel, a backstreet in the Vedado district of Havana, into an open-air art gallery. The walls and houses of the alley are covered with large, brightly colored murals adorned with Santeria symbols. Born in Camagüey, González Escalona began painting in 1960, but he didn't have a public show of his art until 1980.

HATUEY (?–1511) Hatuey was a powerful Taino chief who fled to Cuba from Hispaniola after the Carib Indians conquered that island. Hatuey led the Taino resistance against the Spanish in Cuba, but he and his followers were captured in 1511 and sentenced to be burned at the stake. A monk offered to baptize Hatuey as a Christian so that his soul would be saved. Hatuey refused, declaring that a heaven populated by Spanish Christians held no attraction for him.

JOSÉ MARTÍ (1853–1895) Cuban national hero José Martí was born to Spanish immigrant parents in Havana. His first political essay, published when he was a sixteen-year-old high school student, led to his conviction for treason and deportation to Spain. In Spain he was educated as a lawyer, but he returned to Cuba and continued to speak out for Cuban independence. After a second deportation to Spain in 1879, Martí moved to New York City. There he continued to write poetry and essays until he traveled to Cuba in 1895 to lead the Second War of Independence. He was killed in a skirmish just days after the war began.

TEÓFILO STEVENSON (b. 1952) A heavyweight boxer from Puerto Padre in northeastern Cuba, Stevenson was the first boxer ever to win gold in three consecutive Olympics, in 1972, 1976, and 1980. He made history by refusing to move to the United States and turn professional. He turned down an offer of $5 million to fight world heavyweight champion Muhammad Ali, saying, "What is $5 million worth when I have the love of 5 million Cubans?" He prefers to stay in Cuba and train a new generation of boxers.

Most travel to Cuba is illegal for U.S. citizens. Exceptions to the travel ban include travelers who visit for humanitarian reasons, relatives of Cubans, and journalists.

CAPITOLIO A copy of the U.S. Capitol in Washington, D.C., the former seat of the Cuban Congress in Havana houses the Cuban Academy of Sciences and the National Library of Science and Technology.

CASTILLO DE SAN PEDRO DEL MORRO This baroque fort near Santiago de Cuba is considered the best-preserved seventeenth-century Spanish military complex in the Caribbean. It creates an imposing presence at the entrance to the harbor, looking out over the Caribbean Sea from atop a 197-foot-high (60-m) cliff.

GRAN PARQUE NATURAL DE MONTEMAR This national park, a vast, mangrove-filled wetland of marshes and swamps near the Bay of Pigs, is home to 160 species of birds, 31 species of reptiles, and 12 species of mammals. It also provides sanctuary for many unusual and endangered species.

LA HABANA VIEJA Old Havana is the original city founded by the Spanish in 1519 on the banks of the Havana harbor. Its narrow cobbled streets are brimming with five hundred years of history, packed into dozens of colonial buildings.

ISLA DE LA JUVENTUD (ISLE OF YOUTH) During the 1500s through the 1700s, Cuba's largest offshore island was a popular hideout for pirates. The island was the inspiration for British author Robert Louis Stevenson's renowned novel *Treasure Island.* Since the revolution, the island has become a center of education for Cuban youth. The island's name, the Isle of Youth, stems from this activity.

JARDÍN BOTÁNICO SOLEDAD The 232-acre (94-hectare) botanical garden in Cienfuegos is the largest in Cuba and has more than two thousand species of plants from around the world, including three hundred varieties of palms.

blockade: to surround an enemy country or area with troops or warships to prevent passage of people or supplies

Communism: a political and economic system in which community resources are owned jointly and shared equally by the whole community

coral reef: a ridge of rocklike formations made up of billions of coral polyp skeletons. Large accumulations of coral can turn into small islands.

mangrove: a tropical tree that grows in swamps and coastal areas. The tree's unique prop roots grow outward from the stem, stabilizing the plant and binding it to the soil.

nationalization: a government buying or seizing privately owned businesses and property and placing them under government ownership

New World: the Western hemisphere (North and South America)

paladares: restaurants operated in private Cuban homes. The restaurants are not allowed to seat more than twelve guests. Owners are allowed to purchase food items (for their guests only) that are not available to other Cubans.

private enterprise: also called free enterprise, the freedom of private individuals or companies to do business without government interference

rain forest: a wet, humid forest populated by tall evergreen trees with leaves that form a continuous canopy (the topmost layer of leaves)

rationing: providing food and consumer goods in fixed quantities at certain specified times

sanctions: economic or military measures intended to punish a nation or force it to do something

Santeria: the major Afro-Cuban religion, which represents a blend of Yoruba and Roman Catholic beliefs and saints. Gods and goddesses in Santeria are called orishas.

son: music that originated in the Sierra Maestra of eastern Cuba in the 1800s. A blend of African rhythms and Spanish melodies, son may be played on a variety of instruments, but the traditional son band includes tres (three-stringed guitar), guitar, trumpet, bongo, guiro, and vocals.

trade embargo: a government order forbidding the export and import of goods to and from a country or territory

trade winds: tropical winds that blow toward the equator from high-pressure areas. Trade winds blow from the northeast in the Northern Hemisphere and from the southeast in the Southern Hemisphere.

tropic of Cancer: an imaginary line running around the globe 23½ degrees north of the equator. The Tropics make up an area of the globe that lies between the tropic of Cancer and the tropic of Capricorn (23½ degrees south of the equator). The Tropics experience mild weather year round.

urbanization: the change from a community with a small population to a city with a large population, which may put a strain on services necessary to support that population

Glossary

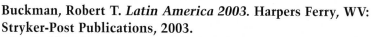

Buckman, Robert T. *Latin America 2003.* Harpers Ferry, WV: Stryker-Post Publications, 2003.
The World Today series contains concise, current information on the countries of the world, including Cuba, and covers history, geography, economy, culture, and current affairs. It is updated annually.

Chapman, Charles E. *A History of the Cuban Republic.* New York: Octagon Books, 1969.
This book provides a detailed history of Cuba up to the formation of the independent Republic of Cuba and its early years.

CIA: The World Factbook: Cuba. N.d.
<http://www.odci.gov/cia/publications/factbook/geos/cu.html>
This site includes updated information and statistics on Cuba's geography, population, economy, government, communications, transportation, military, and transnational issues.

The Europa World Yearbook 2001. London: Europa Publications Limited, 2001.
This annual publication includes statistics on everything from agriculture and tourism to education and population density. It also contains a detailed account of Cuba's history and current events, government, military, economy, social welfare, and education, as well as a list of public holidays.

Foner, Philip S. *A History of Cuba and Its Relations with the United States.* New York: International Publishers, 1962.
This two-volume work is a thorough examination of the history of Cuba from its first contact with Europeans in 1492 to the Second War of Independence in 1895.

Harrington, M. R. *Cuba before Columbus.* New York: Museum of the American Indian, 1921.
This two-volume account of archaeological findings from Cuba provides insights into the people who inhabited the island before the arrival of the Europeans.

Population Reference Bureau. 2003.
<http://www.prb.org/> (October 24, 2003)
The annual statistics on this site provide a wealth of data on Cuba's population, birth and death rates, fertility rate, infant mortality rate, and other useful demographic information.

Simons, Geoff. *Cuba: From Conquistador to Castro.* New York: St. Martin's Press, 1996.
Through an exploration of government and nongovernment documents, media reports, and books, as well as several visits to Cuba, the author presents an unbiased analysis of Cuban politics and social structure.

Stanley, David. *Cuba.* Melbourne, Australia: Lonely Planet Publications, 2000.
This travel guide to Cuba contains detailed information on provinces, major cities and towns, attractions, and events, as well as the history, geography, economy, natural history, and culture of the country.

Suchlicki, Jaime. *Cuba: From Columbus to Castro.* New York: Scribner, 1974.
This work offers a concise account of post-Columbian Cuban history up until Castro's revolution.

Tattlin, Isadora. *Cuba Diaries: An American Housewife in Havana.* Chapel Hill, NC: Algonquin Books of Chapel Hill, 2002.
The author reveals firsthand information on everyday life in Cuba, drawing from diary entries she kept during the four years she lived there during the mid-1990s.

Thomas, Hugh. *Cuba: The Pursuit of Freedom.* New York: Harper & Row, 1971.
In this nearly two-thousand-page book, the author chronicles two centuries of Cuban history. He begins with the British temporary takeover of Cuba in 1762 and ends with the new republic's increasing ties to the Soviet Union in 1962.

United Nations Statistics Division. 2002.
<http://www.un.org/Depts/unsd/> (October 24, 2003)
This site offers a wide range of statistics on Cuba, including economic, environmental, social, and demographic data.

Williams, Byron. *Cuba: The Continuing Revolution.* New York: Parents' Magazine Press, 1969.
This is an excellent, unbiased look at the People's Revolution in Cuba and U.S. policies toward Cuba. The book outlines the hardships caused as a result of U.S. intervention, as well as the restraints inflicted on Cubans in the first decade of the Castro regime.

AfroCubaWeb
<http://afrocubaweb.com>

This website devoted to the influence of African cultures in Cuba provides a wealth of current information about Afro-Cuban music, religion, and arts.

Behnke, Alison, and Victor Manuel Valens. *Cooking the Cuban Way.* Minneapolis: Lerner Publications Company, 2004.

This informative cookbook describes the cuisine and culture of Cuba and offers recipes for main courses, side dishes, desserts, and holiday and festival foods, including vegetarian options.

Crouch, Clifford W. *Cuba.* Philadelphia: Chelsea House Publishers, 1999.

This book is a comprehensive look at Cuba's history, geography, economy, and social life.

CubanCulture
<http://www.cubanculture.com>

This website about Cubans and their unique culture includes information about Cuban art, music, literature, and cuisine.

CubaNet
<http://www.cubanet.org/cubanews.html>

This website collects articles from many different sources to provide current information and news about Cuba.

García, Cristina. *The Agüero Sisters.* New York: Knopf, 1997.

This novel depicts the different lives of two Cuban sisters, one who lives in Cuba and one who lives in the United States.

———. *Dreaming in Cuban.* New York: Knopf, 1992.

This novel centers on three generations of Cuban women with different experiences. The grandmother lives in Cuba permanently, her daughter grows up in Cuba and moves to the United States as a young woman, and the granddaughter moves to the United States soon after birth and grows up there.

Griffiths, John. *The Cuban Missile Crisis.* Vero Beach, FL: Rourke, 1987.

This detailed account describes the Cuban Missile Crisis of 1962 and the events that led up to it.

Hemingway, Ernest. *The Old Man and the Sea.* New York: Scribner, 1952.

One of Hemingway's finest works, this is a touching novel about an old Cuban fisherman and the sea that is his life.

Jacobs, Francine. *The Tainos: The People Who Welcomed Columbus.* New York: G. P. Putnam's Sons, 1992.

In this insightful book, Jacobs traces the history of the Taino people from their first encounter with Columbus to their extinction a few decades later.

Morrison, Marion. *Cuba: City and Village Life.* Austin, TX: Steck-Vaughn, 1998.

The author describes the economic and social life of Cuba, with an emphasis on the differences between life in the city and in the country.

Suchlicki, Jaime. *Historical Dictionary of Cuba.* **2nd ed. London: The Scarecrow Press, 2001.**
This reference book contains a wealth of information on Cuba, from personalities to historical and current events.

vgsbooks.com
<http://www.vgsbooks.com>
Visit vgsbooks.com, the homepage of the Visual Geography Series®. You can get linked to all sorts of useful online information, including geographical, historical, demographic, cultural, and economic websites. The vgsbooks.com site is a great resource for late-breaking news and statistics.

Yip, Dora, and Mark Cramer. *Welcome to Cuba.* **Milwaukee: Gareth Stevens, 2001.**
This book focuses on social life in Cuba, including culture, sports, and religion.

African heritage, 17, 45, 48, 49–50, 54, 72
Afro-Cuban Allstars, 49
Afro-Cubans, 17, 21, 46, 48, 71, 72; religions of, 45, 70
agriculture. *See* farming
Alonso, Alicia, 50, 70
animals, 12–14, 15
architecture, 15, 16, 17, 51–52
arts and crafts, 16, 19, 44, 50–51, 71

Batista, Fulgencio, 70; rule of, 27, 28, 29
Bay of Pigs invasion, 31
Buena Vista Social Club, 49, 71

Camagüey, 17, 20, 51
Caribbean nations, 8, 23, 36
Carnival, 46, 72
cars, 14, 60, 64
Castro, Fidel, 4, 7, 28–35, 65, 70; ideology of, 5, 28, 30, 32; leads revolution, 28–29; repression under, 32, 65; view of United States, 5, 30, 34, 65
Catholicism, 21, 33, 44–45
cigars, 14, 61, 62
cities, 15–17, 20, 46, 72
climate, 10, 12
Columbus, Christopher, 19–20
Communism, 4–5, 65; definition of, 4–5, 30
community service, 43
Cuba: boundaries and location, 4, 8; climate, 10, 12; constitution, 26, 32, 34, 45; currency, 68; flag, 13, 26, 69; flora and fauna, 12–14, 72; government, 4–5, 27, 34–35; maps, 6, 11; national anthem, 69; population, 7, 15, 36
Cuban Communist Party (PCC), 35
Cuban missile crisis, 31–32
Cuban revolution. *See* People's Revolution.
currency, 68; foreign, 57, 59

economy, 5, 7, 14, 33, 56–65; colonial, 21, 22, 23, 24, 25; dollar stores, 39. *See also* sugar
education, 14, 32, 42–43, 48, 52; Isle of Youth, 43, 72

embargo, U.S., 5, 30, 40, 56, 63, 65
emigration and exile, 31, 32–33, 34, 36, 48, 57, 71
energy and fuel, 14, 33, 60, 64
environment, 12, 14–15; tourism and, 14, 59
ethnic groups, 4, 7, 17, 23, 36–37. *See also* indigenous peoples
exports, 14, 60, 62, 63

family life, 41, 44
farming, 12, 14, 43, 54, 60–61; colonial, 20–21, 23; postrevolutionary, 32, 57, 60–61; pre-Columbian, 19
fishes and fishing, 13, 14, 16, 18, 54
food, 7, 12, 14, 38, 47, 54–55; rationing, 33, 38–39; recipe, 54; restaurants, 58
foreign relations, 5, 30, 34, 43, 56, 58
French colonies, 16–17, 22

Grau San Martín, Ramón, 27
Guantánamo naval base, 26
Guevara, Ernesto "Che," 28–29

Haiti, 8, 16–17, 22
harbors and ports, 7, 10, 15, 17, 21
Havana, 15–16, 20, 25, 29, 37, 46; Old Havana, 15, 16
health and health care, 14, 21, 28, 32, 38, 39–41; tourism and, 59
Helms-Burton Act, 63
Hemingway, Ernest, 48
history: Batista regime, 27–28; conquistadores, 19–21; People's Revolution, 4, 7, 28–29; independence, 26–27; post-revolution, 4–5, 7, 32–34; pre-Columbian, 4, 18–19, 50; Second War of Independence, 24–26; Spanish colonization, 4, 19–24, 51
holidays and festivals, 46–47
housing, 7, 16, 19, 37–38, 41, 51
human rights and freedoms, 31, 32, 33, 35, 45, 46, 65
hurricanes, 12

independence, struggles for, 24–25, 47, 70; literature about, 47 indigenous peoples, 18–19, 20, 36, 50; Arawak, 4, 18, 20; Taino, 4, 19, 20, 51, 53, 71

industry and manufacturing, 14, 16, 17, 46, 61–62

Isla de la Juventud (Isle of Youth), 9–10, 21, 43, 50, 72

islands, 8, 9–10, 15

Jews, Cuban, 46

John Paul II (pope), 33, 45

Kennedy, John F., 31

Krushchev, Nikita, 31–32

land reform, 32, 60–61

language, 4, 19, 46, 47

literacy, 42

literature and writers, 33, 47, 70, 71

Machado, Gerardo, 27

maps, 6, 11

Martí, José, 24, 46, 47, 72

medicine and pharmaceuticals, 59, 61–62

minerals and mining, 14, 20, 56, 60; gold, 20; nickel, 14, 56, 60

mountains, 9, 12

music and dance, 17, 46, 47, 48–50, 70, 71

nationalization, 30, 56

natural resources, 14

Pan American Games, 53–54

People's Revolution, 4, 7, 28–29, 48; achievements of, 32, 39, 41, 42, 48, 52, 65; goals of, 30, 32, 39, 42, 60

pirates, 21, 72

Platt Amendment, 26, 27

political parties, 26, 35

private enterprise (business), 30, 33, 57, 58

rainfall, 10, 12

rationing, 7, 33, 38

religion, 21, 32, 33, 44–46, 47, 70, 71

rivers and lakes, 10

Santeria, 45–46; orishas, 45–46

Santiago de Cuba, 16–17, 46, 72

ships and shipping, 21, 22

slaves and slavery, 16, 17, 20–21, 22, 23, 24; culture of, 45, 46, 48, 72

social classes, 23–24, 28, 59

social services, 7, 14; under Batista, 28; under Castro, 32, 39–43

Soviet Union (USSR), 5, 7, 30, 31, 32, 33, 52, 56, 63; collapse of, 7, 33, 56

Spanish rule, 4, 15, 16, 17, 20–25, 51

Special Period in Peacetime, 33, 54

sports, 52–54, 70; baseball, 53; Olympic Games, 53–54

standard of living, 7, 16, 28, 37–39

sugar, 14, 27, 28, 30, 32, 46, 72; economics of, 56, 59–60, 61; slavery and, 22, 23, 46; sugarcane, 60

tourism, 14, 15, 28, 33, 40; economics of, 56, 58–59; sights to see, 72

trade, 7, 62–63; colonial, 21, 22, 23; foreign trade, 5, 33, 38, 56, 62–63. *See also* embargo, U.S.

transportation, 7, 63–64

United States, 23, 39; economy of, 30; emigration to, 31, 32–33, 34, 36, 48, 71; influence of, 52; occupation of Cuba, 25–26; relations with Cuba, 5, 7, 24, 27, 30–31, 40, 69, 72. *See also* embargo, U.S.

USS *Maine*, 25

Varela Project, 35

Velázquez, Diego, 20, 51

wars and conflicts, 22, 31; People's Revolution, 4, 7, 28–29; Second War of Independence, 24–26; Seven Years' War, 22; Spanish-American War, 25–26; Ten Years' War (First War of Independence), 24, 46, 69

water, 10, 28, 38

women, 41, 44

work and workers, 28, 32, 41, 56, 61; colonial, 20–21, 23–24; salaries of, 38, 56; sugar and, 59–60

Yoruba culture, 45

Captions for photos appearing on cover and chapter openers:

Cover: A rural house in western Cuba

pp. 4–5 The fort known as El Castillo de los Tres Reyes de Magos del Morro (also called El Morro) overlooks the picturesque Havana harbor.

pp. 8–9 The Viñales Valley in the Cordillera de Guaniguanico in Pinar del Río province boasts some of the most beautiful inland scenery in Cuba, including mogotes, straight-sided rocks that rise abruptly from the surrounding land.

pp. 18–19 These petroglyphs (carvings on stone) were carved by the Taino Indians on the island of Puerto Rico. The Taino fled from Puerto Rico and other Caribbean islands to Cuba around A.D. 1250, when another indigenous group attacked them. For links to more information on the history of the Taino, visit www.vgsbooks.com.

pp. 36–37 These children reflect some of the varied ethnic and racial backgrounds of modern Cubans.

pp. 44–45 Families are important in Cuba and often include several generations living together.

pp. 56–57 Cubans in Havana shop at a local vegetable market. Agriculture has been the base of Cuba's economy since the Spanish first arrived in the early 1500s. These days, small, privately owned farms provide a reliable source of income for farmers and offer affordable, fresh produce for customers.

Photo Acknowledgments

The images in this book are used with the permission of: © Superstock, pp. 4–5; © Ron Bell/Digital Cartographics, pp, 6, 11; © TRIP/J. Highet, pp. 8–9; © John R. Kreul/Independent Picture Service, pp. 10, 13 (bottom), 52, 59, 61; © TRIP/ K. Cardwell, pp. 13 (top), 16–17; © Harry Lerner/Independent Picture Service, pp. 14, 15, 39, 40, 42, 47, 48, 50–51 (bottom), 63, 64; © Stephanie Maze/ CORBIS, pp. 18–19; James Ford Bell Library, University of Minnesota, p. 20; © Bettmann/CORBIS, pp. 22, 30, 31; Library of Congress, p. 23 (USZ62-096628); © Hulton-Deutsch Collection/CORBIS, p. 27; © Robert M. Levine, p. 29; © Getty Images, pp. 33, 34, 35; © AFP/CORBIS, p. 35; © Sam Lund, pp. 36–37, 44–45, 58; © Ed Quinn/CORBIS, p. 38; © Philip Bourns, p. 41; © Bill Gentile/CORBIS, p. 43; © Art Directors/TRIP/Michael O'Brien, pp. 49; © Reuters NewMedia Inc./CORBIS, pp. 50 (top), 53; © Walter & Louiseann Pietrowicz/September 8th Stock, p. 55; © TRIP/M. Barlow, pp. 56–57; © TRIP/M. O'Brien, p. 62; © AFP/Getty Images, p. 65; © www.banknotes.com, p. 68.

Cover photo: © John R. Kreul/Independent Picture Service. Back cover: © NASA.